LEARNING TO LIVE WITH EVIL

LEARNING
TO LIVE
WITH EVIL

by
THEODORE   PLANTINGA

WILLIAM B. EERDMANS
PUBLISHING COMPANY   GRAND RAPIDS

Library of Congress Cataloging in Publication Data

Plantinga, Theodore, 1947-
Learning to live with evil.
Includes index.
1.   Good and evil.   2.   Providence and government of
God.   I.   Title.
BJ1401.P58   231'.8   81-22041
ISBN 0-8028-1917-6   AACR2

We gratefully acknowledge the permission of the publisher and the author to quote
from John Hick's *Evil and the God of Love* (New York: Harper and Row, 1978).

The method of averting one's attention from evil, and living simply in the light of good, is splendid as long as it will work. It will work with many persons; it will work far more generally than most of us are ready to suppose; and within the sphere of its successful operation there is nothing to be said against it as a religious solution. But it breaks down impotently as soon as melancholy comes; and even though one be quite free from melancholy one's self, there is no doubt that healthy-mindedness is inadequate as a philosophical doctrine, because the evil facts which it refuses positively to account for are a genuine portion of reality; and they may after all be the best key to life's significance, and possibly the only openers of our eyes to the deepest levels of truth.

—WILLIAM JAMES,
The Varieties of Religious Experience

CONTENTS

PREFACE

THIS book, which grew out of a course on evil that I taught at Calvin College, has a dual purpose. In the first place, it is intended to acquaint readers with the major views on evil that have developed within and alongside the Christian tradition. As much as possible, I have allowed thinkers and commentators to speak for themselves instead of summing up their ideas in words of my own. In the second place, the book argues a thesis in opposition to one of the views of evil discussed (i.e., evil as non-being). My thesis is that the failure of this position to take evil seriously leads to certain consequences that are unacceptable from a Biblical point of view. By way of example, I have focused briefly on approaches to education and the punishment of criminals.

A feature that distinguishes the book from other treatments of evil is the discussion of man's abiding preoccupation with various manifestations of evil. (Here I could almost speak of a universal human *fascination* with evil.) Part of the purpose of the course from which the book arose was to explore such questions as: Must we always avert our eyes from manifestations of evil? Can the beholding of evil ever edify us? Ought evil to be depicted? Are there any circumstances in which we are obliged to confront evil with its ugliness instead of turning away from it? In the book I have offered answers to such questions.

As I showed the manuscript to friends and colleagues to elicit commentary and critique, I found that my title quickly gave rise to certain questions. Hence a word of explanation is in order. When I suggest that we must learn to live with evil, I do not mean to counsel an attitude of resignation, as if there could be no point in resisting or opposing evil. Rather, the conclusion I offer is that the presence of evil in this world — including both sickness and sin — must be understood as a consequence of man's rebellion against God. In short, God's hand of judgment still rests on our lives. Once we realize that we may not ignore evil or seek to explain it away but must learn to live with it in this interim age, we will yearn with all our hearts for the final triumph of the Kingdom of God on that great day when evil is fully overcome and all our tears are wiped away.

INTRODUCTION

I

DISCUSSIONS of the problem of evil generally begin on a somber note. Many of them end on a somber note as well. Often an investigation of the dark side of life succeeds only in making the shadows longer.

It sometimes seems that treatments of the problem of evil are either statements of a gloomy pessimism or expressions of the laughable optimism that Voltaire made fun of in *Candide*. Yet this impression is not entirely accurate. In discussions of evil we usually hear fundamental questions being raised, questions to which answers are not easily found. Why is there suffering? If there is a God, why does He permit so much suffering? For what purpose do I exist? Why should I go on existing?

Indeed, why go on? The classic form of this question is: Why even be born? The German writer Lessing, responding to the death of his infant son, wrote some harsh, chilling words, words in which sarcasm and pain are mingled:

> My joy was short-lived. And it pained me so to lose him — this son. For he had so much sense, so much sense! . . . Wasn't it good sense on his part that they had to drag him into the world with iron tongs, and that he so quickly recognized the world's wretchedness? Wasn't it sense that he seized the first opportunity to escape from it? And the little rascal even takes his mother away with him![1]

Arthur Schopenhauer, a German philosopher famous for his pessimism and witty sarcasm, has spoken out in the same vein:

> But as regards the life of the individual, every life-history is a history of suffering, for, as a rule, every life is a continual series of mishaps great and small, concealed as much as possible by everyone, because he knows that others are almost always bound to feel satisfaction at the spectacle of annoyances from which they are for the moment exempt; rarely will they feel sympathy or compassion. But perhaps at the end of his life, no man, if he be sincere and at the same time in possession of his faculties, will ever wish to go through it again.

Rather than this, he will much prefer to choose complete non-existence. The essential purport of the world-famous monologue in *Ham-
let* [To be or not to be . . .] is, in condensed form, that our state is so
wretched that complete non-existence would be decidedly preferable
to it.[2]

There are times when we feel there may be something to such
pessimistic talk. It is one thing to be young and in love, but quite
another to be burdened with the infirmities and indignities of old
age. David Hume observed:

That Suicide may often be consistent with interest and with our
duty to ourselves, no one can question, who allows that age, sickness,
or misfortune, may render life a burden, and make it worse even than
annihilation. I believe that no man ever threw away life while it was
worth keeping.[3]

For some people the time does come when life no longer seems
worth keeping. Henry P. Van Dusen, an eminent churchman,
shocked much of the world by carrying out a suicide pact with his
wife in 1975. He was 77, and she was 80.

What does it mean to commit suicide? The act of suicide can
be viewed as a response to the problem of evil — a personal or
existential response. For many, it is an affirmation of the shocking
proposition that *nothing* is better than something.

There have been a number of theoretical (i.e., theological and
philosophical) responses to the problem of evil, but the problem
is not first of all — or even primarily — theoretical in nature.
Evil confronts us with choices to be made; it demands a response
involving much more than intellect. And one response people offer
is sheer denial. They declare that it is better to die than to live,
and that it would be better still never to be born at all. Many
translate these words into deeds by committing suicide.

The strategy of denial as a response to the problem of evil also
comes to expression in other ways. Evil can be so painful to confront that the only thing left to do is to hide from it — by pre-
tending that evil is not evil. For a few, this strategy takes the form
of a superficial optimism, but most people who deny evil move on
to the next step and deny good as well.

Those who do so are offering a response to evil, a response that
is existential as well as (implicitly) theoretical. In John Steinbeck's
gripping novel *The Grapes of Wrath* we meet Casy, the lapsed

preacher who wrestles with his own sinfulness and the enormity of the frightening changes coming over the land. The preacher drops the word *sin* from his vocabulary: "There ain't no sin and there ain't no virtue. There's just stuff people do. It's all part of the same thing. And some of the things folks do is nice, and some ain't nice, but that's as far as any man got a right to say."[4]

II

The strategy of denial as a response to the problem of evil is all around us. Almost as widespread is another response, which we might call the "anesthetic" approach.

We all know what anesthetic is from our visits to the dentist. I have been under local anesthetic when work was done on my teeth, but I have also gone without. There's quite a difference. I have relied on anesthetic when a cut was closed with stitches, and I have also had stitches without. And in this case the difference is even greater.

An anesthetic desensitizes us; it renders us incapable of feeling pain. When the dentist approaches with his drill, most of us want an injection of painkiller first. Yet there are people who do not shrink from the pain that could be spared them. Many women, for example, choose natural childbirth. In another sort of experience entirely, some people succumb to dreaded diseases with little or no medication to help them cope with the pain.

I don't believe we should discourage people who choose to do so from availing themselves of the anesthetics doctors provide. Still, there is something to be learned from the example of those who face pain unaided, for the use of anesthetics can be dangerous.

During earlier centuries, many soldiers had wounded arms or legs amputated. Anesthetics were not available; the suffering soldiers were given stiff doses of whiskey before the operation to somewhat deaden the pain.

Whiskey, of course, is no longer used in our society as a painkiller during surgery, but it is certainly popular among people who take the anesthetic approach to evil. Millions of people in our time drink their problems away, or use drugs to bring about the same numbing effect.

The states they achieve resemble certain conditions which the body can induce within itself. A person who is confronted with the death of a loved one may go into shock; he may become numb for some time, thereby giving himself a chance to get used to the horrible reality he faces. At times the enormity of evil is so great that we are literally unable to confront it. This would seem to indicate that the anesthetic approach should not be entirely scorned.

Some people manage to adopt the anesthetic posture without relying on liquor, drugs, or medicine. They do so by systematically holding their feelings in check. They stifle the impulse to sympathize with their fellow human beings; they train themselves to be hard, unfeeling, uncaring. Some even elevate insensitivity to a virtue! They forget that insensitivity to others ultimately becomes insensitivity to oneself.

III

I do not recommend either denial or anesthesia as responsible approaches to evil. Both are understandable, and most of us have flirted with one or the other — if not both. Still, both are to be rejected, for there are words of hope that can be spoken as we ponder the presence of evil in our lives.

Christian believers who live close to the Bible know that their reflection — both existential and theoretical — must begin with God's Word. When God's people in Biblical times faced danger and oppression, they knew what to ask: "Is there any word from the Lord?" (Jeremiah 37:17). We must remember to ask the same question. We should not await a prophet with a new revelation but should turn to the written revelation of God to see what light it sheds on the problem of evil.

The Biblical message about evil is that it is a reality which we may not ignore or deny. We are to confront it squarely — both existentially and theoretically — and learn to live with it in this interim age between the first and second comings of Christ.

This is not to say that the Bible answers all our questions about evil. Those who have lost loved ones and those who suffer from chronic infirmities know that painful questions can linger in human hearts year in and year out. Sin and evil remain mysterious for the believer.

The familiar emphasis on "faith seeking understanding" can help us in our reflection on evil. The Word of God has some things to say about sin and evil — about sin's beginning, its persistence among us, and the measures we must take to keep it at bay. As we increase in spiritual maturity and wisdom, the Bible's guidance concerning evil becomes more understandable. Yet the standpoint of faith seeking understanding is never left behind in this life. We look forward to the day when our faith will attain the clarity of sight.

IV

How can we best proceed in discussing evil? It seems to me that we should begin with some reflection on the major types or categories of evil — natural, moral, and demonic (Part I). With such material before us, we will look at some of the major theories regarding evil, paying special attention to what leading Christian thinkers have said (Part II). The perspective that emerges should help us draw some practical, down-to-earth conclusions about the evil around us, for example, evil in such forms as pornography, violence, suffering, and conflict. Must we always avert our eyes when we come upon evil, or are there situations that call for us to behold evil (Part III)? Finally, we should ask how our longing for Christ's return might help us deal with the presence of evil in this world. What does the coming of God's Kingdom into this world imply for education and for our attitude toward punishment? Must we conclude that God's judgment on sinful humanity is a major factor in the web of evil around us (Part IV)?

PART ONE

TYPES
OF
EVIL

SIN often does battle with sickness when lawyers lock horns in our courtrooms. If the criminal is a sinner, a willful transgressor, he should be punished, but if he is suffering from a sickness, he should be treated in a hospital and should not be held responsible for the damage or injury he has caused.

Two rival conceptions of evil are at war here. Can they be reconciled? To be able to discuss this question, we must look at the types of evil.

In most schemes there are two types of evil: natural (or physical) evil and moral evil. I propose to add a third type: demonic evil, which falls within the domain of moral evil in many other schemes and is denied outright in some. There are also thinkers who distinguish natural evil from something they call metaphysical imperfection (by which they mean an inadequacy in the very constitution of things and persons), but I see no need for such a distinction.

The reasoning supporting this threefold division will become clear in the course of the exposition. I will characterize the types of evil in the three chapters that make up Part I; my account of the interrelations between them will come in Chapter 8, with which Part II concludes.

CHAPTER ONE

NATURAL EVIL

I

NATURAL evil affects man insofar as he is a part of nature and thereby subject to the same sorts of perils and afflictions to which animals fall prey. Animals are buried in avalanches — and so are people. Animals perish in forest fires — and so do people. Animals die of diseases — and so do people. All these ills are regrettable; yet it appears that there is no one to hold responsible.

We find a classic characterization of natural evil in David Hume's *Dialogues Concerning Natural Religion.* The ills listed by Hume apply especially to the animal realm, but man is not left out:

> The whole Earth . . . is curst and polluted. A perpetual War is kindled amongst all living Creatures. Necessity, Hunger, Want stimulate the strong and courageous: Fear, Anxiety, Terror agitate the weak and infirm. The first Entrance into Life gives Anguish to the new-born Infant and to its wretched Parent: Weakness, Impotence, Distress attend each Stage of that Life: And 'tis at last finish'd in Agony and Horror.
>
> Observe too . . . the curious Artifices of Nature, in order to imbitter the Life of every living Being. The stronger prey upon the weaker, and keep them in perpetual Terror and Anxiety. The weaker too, in their turn, often prey upon the stronger, and vex and molest them without Relaxation. Consider that innumerable Race of Insects, which either are bred on the Body of each Animal, or flying about infix their Stings in him. These Insects have others still less than themselves, which torment them. And thus on each hand, before and behind, above and below, every Animal is surrounded with Enemies, which incessantly seek his Misery and Destruction.[1]

As we contemplate fearful nature and her ways, the torments and forms of death she inflicts seem downright criminal. The analogy with crime occurred to John Stuart Mill as he wrote his essay on nature. We read:

> In sober truth, nearly all the things which men are hanged or imprisoned for doing to one another, are nature's every day performances. Killing, the most criminal act recognized by human laws, Nature does once to every being that lives; and in a large proportion of cases, after protracted tortures such as only the greatest monsters whom we read of ever purposely inflicted on their living fellow-creatures. . . . Nature impales men, breaks them as if on the wheel, casts them to be devoured by wild beasts, burns them to death, crushes them with stones like the first christian martyr, starves them with hunger, freezes them with cold, poisons them by the quick or slow venom of her exhalations, and has hundreds of other hideous deaths in reserve.[2]

II

Much, perhaps too much, has been written about the ills and woes that fall under the heading of natural evil. Therefore I must begin by noting that not everything called natural evil is rightly regarded as evil. S. Paul Schilling claims that accidental deaths entail "unfulfilled potentialities." A young woman who has suffered brain death but lingers on in a coma might have been able to contribute much to society, but her potential will never be fulfilled.[3]

True, such a tragedy is a loss in many ways, but we should be careful not to multiply our woes needlessly. Whether we are discussing a living person or a dead person, a potential that was never developed should not be thought of as a reality that once existed and then was destroyed. The fact of the matter is that it has no more reality than the elusive money which we are supposed to be able to "save up" for some purpose or other by taking advantage of bargains.

Suppose I want to take a vacation and need to save up the money first. Would I then go to the local furniture store's anniversary sale and buy new furniture? I might save $200 on a couch, $100 on a bed, and so forth. But I would not walk out with $300 "saved up," which I could then set aside for the vacation. Money "saved" for a trip is money earned and not spent. The money I "saved" at the furniture store is not money that can be spent; it is money I never had.

Likewise, potentials that I have never developed are not to be regarded as possessions that were somehow taken away from me, leaving me diminished. A normal human being is potentially capable of such a wide range of abilities and skills that in choosing *for* some he cannot help choosing *against* others. We should rejoice in the potentials we are able to develop — and not agonize over what might have been.

However, there is a genuine loss, which we correctly regard as an evil, when an existing talent is lost or destroyed through injury or disease. If the hands of a pianist are crushed in an accident, for example, we have reason to regard the accident as an evil occurrence. Naturally, there is also something wrong when a person neglects the development of talents and abilities, but here we are in the domain of moral evil or sin rather than natural evil.

III

To avoid making more of natural evil than we ought, we must remember that the world (including nature) was created good. And despite the fall into sin with its consequences, we may still speak of this earth as God's good creation and give thanks for it.

Yet, to say that it is good is not to claim that it is perfect. There is a good deal of confusion about the concept of perfection. The roots of this concept lie in metaphysical speculation, that is, in abstract philosophical reasoning about being. Two aspects of perfection as it is traditionally understood have caused special confusion with regard to natural evil. First of all, perfection is identified with fullness. Second, it is thought that being perfect means being like God. Let's look at the second of these aspects first.

Man was created good; that is to say, he was perfect in the ordinary sense — complete, with nothing missing, like a newborn baby pronounced "perfect" by the attending physician. The animals and plants were likewise created good. God created them according to their "kinds." This means that a snail is a snail — and not a frog. A frog, likewise, is not a human being. And a human being is not God.

This seems straightforward enough, but some thinkers have interpreted this state of affairs differently. Starting from the notion of a hierarchy of being, they decided that the frog is higher than the snail, while man is higher than the frog. God, of course, is higher than man. From here it is but a short step to the idea that the snail would be better if it were a frog. As for man, he may possess a relative goodness, but he would be better yet if he were God.

At this point we must simply shake our heads and say that it is good for each creature to be what it is. There is no inherent evil in the frog's being a frog, although there is indeed an evil in a frog's being without legs. Likewise, a human being may not complain about being a mere human rather than a deity; there is nothing evil about his being a human being, although natural evil is evident if a human being lacks, for example, arms and legs.

Those who conceive of perfection as fullness confuse divine and human attributes. God is unique in that He is not only good but perfect; we attribute complete perfection to Him. He is everything He could be. We do not think in terms of unfulfilled potential in God's case.

We go wrong when we try to argue that man is — or was — good in the same sense. Man is a different kind of being, a being limited in space and time. As I write these words I am in Michigan. It is good to be in Michigan. I know from experience that it is also good to be in Florida, and in Switzerland. But I cannot be in Florida or in Switzerland as long as I am in Michigan. This should not lead us to conclude that there is something inherently evil about being in Michigan.

The difference between male and female should be regarded in similar terms. It is good to be a male. It is also good to be a female. I cannot be a genuine female if I am a male. Still, my not being a female does not make my being a male a manifestation of natural evil.

The point I am trying to express here is closely related to the point made earlier about potentialities. If I choose a full-time career as a teacher, I will not become a full-time nurse, even though it is widely recognized that nursing is interesting and satisfying work. Yet this consideration does not entitle me to conclude that there is something intrinsically wrong with being a teacher.

IV

I have chosen to stress this point because there is a powerful force behind the hankering to be what one is not: Humanism. Humanism is the great rival and opponent of Christianity. It is not simply a philosophy or a worldview that developed at a certain point in

Western civilization; it is the alternative framework for life and thought that pushes God out of the picture and places man at the center.

Humanism feeds on man's discontent. Its message is essentially the message of the tempter in the garden of Eden: "You can become like God. You can erase the boundary between God and yourself."

Much of modern Humanism repeats this alluring claim in one form or another. Humanism, fueled by the sin of pride, entices man to strive for a kind of idealized perfection that ignores his creaturely limitations. We already hear this ideal clearly expressed during the Renaissance era in Pico della Mirandola's *Oration on the Dignity of Man.* The speaker is God, but the message is essentially Satan's challenge to man:

> Neither a fixed abode nor a form that is thine alone nor any function peculiar to thyself have We given thee, Adam, to the end that according to thy longing and according to thy judgment thou mayest have and possess what abode, what form, and what functions thou thyself shalt desire. The nature of all other beings is limited and constrained within the bounds of laws prescribed by Us. Thou, constrained by no limits, in accordance with thine own free will, in whose hand We have placed thee, shalt ordain for thyself the limits of thy nature. . . . Thou shalt have the power to degenerate into the lower forms of life, which are brutish. Thou shalt have the power, out of thy soul's judgment, to be reborn into the higher forms, which are divine.[4]

Much of what some thinkers call natural evil, then, is merely man's rebellion against his own creatureliness, against the status and role God has assigned him. Hence I do not believe we may regard "metaphysical imperfection" as a category of evil in addition to natural evil. We must instead learn to recognize that it is good to be a human being, good to be a male or a female, good to be in Michigan or Florida or Switzerland, good to be a teacher or a nurse.

V

I do not mean to suggest that all the talk about natural evil doesn't amount to much. There is undeniably a great deal of pain and suffering caused by disease and accident. Moreover, nature itself, it seems, is a realm of conflict, of blood and pain and destruction. If you have ever seen a frog and a snake in a cage together and watched the snake take an hour or two to catch the frog and swallow it, you will never forget the sight. Small wonder that we sometimes characterize savagery as "the law of the jungle."

The American novelist Theodore Dreiser was fascinated by natural processes and their meaning. When he wrote a series of three novels based on a single character, Frank Cowperwood, he used a scene much like the encounter between the snake and the frog to set the stage for the conflict that was to unfold in his story:

> There was a fish-market not so very far from his home, and there, on his way to see his father at the bank, or conducting his brothers on after-school expeditions, he liked to look at a certain tank in front of one store where were kept odd specimens of sea-life brought in by the Delaware Bay fishermen. . . . One day he saw a squid and a lobster put in the tank, and in connection with them was witness to a tragedy which stayed with him all his life and cleared things up considerably intellectually. The lobster, it appeared from the talk of the idle by-standers, was offered no food, as the squid was considered his rightful prey. He lay at the bottom of the clear glass tank on the yellow sand, apparently seeing nothing — you could not tell in which way his beady, black buttons of eyes were looking — but apparently they were never off the body of the squid. The latter, pale and waxy in texture, looking very much like pork fat or jade, moved about in torpedo fashion; but his movements were apparently never out of the eyes of his enemy, for by degrees small portions of his body began to disappear, snapped off by the relentless claws of his pursuer. The lobster would leap like a catapult to where the squid was apparently idly dreaming, and the squid, very alert, would dart away, shooting out at the same time a cloud of ink, behind which it would disappear. It was not always completely successful, however. Small portions of its body or its tail were frequently left in the claws of the monster below. Fascinated by the drama young Cowperwood came daily to watch.
>
> One morning he stood in front of the tank, his nose almost pressed to the glass. Only a portion of the squid remained, and his ink-bag was emptier than ever. In the corner of the tank sat the lobster, poised apparently for action.
>
> The boy stayed as long as he could, the bitter struggle fascinating him. Now, maybe, or in an hour or a day, the squid might die, slain by the lobster, and the lobster would eat him. He looked again at the greenish-copperish engine of destruction in the corner and wondered when this would be.[5]

But what is it really like to be a squid being devoured in stages by a lobster? Could it be that we are too free in imagining the horror in the scene Dreiser sketches? The naturalist W. H. Hudson suggests that pain and the fear of death hardly have the impact in the animal world that they have for man:

The "struggle for existence," in so far as animals in a state of nature are concerned, is a metaphorical struggle; and the strife, short and sharp, which is so common in nature, is not misery, although it results in pain, since it is pain that kills or is soon outlived. Fear there is, just as in fine weather there are clouds in the sky; and just as the shadow of the cloud passes, so does fear pass from the wild creature when the object that excited it has vanished from sight. And when death comes, it comes unexpectedly, and is not the death that we know, even before we taste of it, thinking of it with apprehension all our lives long, but a sudden blow that takes away consciousness — the touch of something that numbs the nerves — merely the prick of a needle In whatever way the animal perishes, whether by violence, or excessive cold, or decay, his death is a comparatively easy one. So long as he is fighting with or struggling to escape from an enemy, wounds are not felt as wounds, and scarcely hurt him — as we know from our own experience; and when overcome, if death be not practically instantaneous, as in the case of a small bird seized by a cat, the disabling grip or blow is itself a kind of anodyne, providing insensibility to pain.[6]

We are almost inclined to say that Hudson takes too benign a view of this matter, much as we might wish that what he says were true. Is death really as peaceful as that for animals? Hudson himself, in another book, presents a rather different picture, although we should note that in this latter instance the animal's death comes at the hands of men. Recalling his childhood in South America, he describes how cattle were put to death:

The native manner of killing a cow or bullock at that time was peculiarly painful. Occasionally it would be slaughtered out of sight on the plain, and the hide and flesh brought in by the men, but, as a rule, the beast would be driven up close to the house to save trouble. One of the two or three mounted men engaged in the operation would throw his lasso over the horns, and, galloping off, pull the rope taut; a second man would then drop from his horse, and running up to the animal behind, pluck out his big knife and with two lightning-quick blows sever the tendons of both hind legs. Instantly the beast would go down on his haunches, and the same man, knife in hand, would flit round to its front or side, and, watching his opportunity, presently thrust the long blade into its throat just above the chest, driving it in to the hilt and working it round; then when it was withdrawn a great torrent of blood would pour out from the tortured beast, still standing on his fore-legs, bellowing all the time with agony. At this point the slaughterer would often leap lightly on to its back, stick his spurs in its sides, and, using the flat of his long knife as a whip, pretend to be riding a race, yelling with fiendish glee. The bellowing would subside into deep, awful, sob-like sounds and chokings; then the rider, seeing the animal about to collapse, would fling himself nimbly off.[7]

I have never witnessed such a scene, and I hope I never will. I have seen suffering on the part of animals — enough to convince me that natural evil is not to be treated lightly.

VI

The world is under a curse because of man's fall into sin. As a result, man and animal alike are subject to pain and disease. The pain involved in childbirth — which is a natural process and not an illness — symbolizes the pain that has come into the world through the fall. The Bible even makes a specific reference to the pain to be associated with childbearing because of the fall (Genesis 3:16).

Man has brought the consequences of his rebellion down on the entire creation. As the crown of creation, man was responsible for the world as a whole; its fate was bound up with his. Therefore we read in the Bible that "the whole creation has been groaning in travail" (Romans 8:22).

We do not fully know what to make of such a passage. But part of its meaning, surely, is that animals must now suffer pain that God did not originally intend them to suffer. God's judgment on man's sin and rebellion seems to extend to the animal world.

This is not to say that animals never die peaceful deaths. I believe some of them do, just as some human beings freeze to death peacefully in the bitter cold of winter. All of this may be admitted — provided we recognize that nature is seriously out of joint, and that natural evil is not measured only by pain and suffering.

VII

Fortunately, there is still more to be said. Man was given charge of the earth; he was told to exercise "dominion" over it. The cultural mandate, the task assigned to man, was not withdrawn after the fall.

By virtue of the cultural mandate, man is responsible for keeping natural evil to a minimum and making the earth as habitable as possible for God's creatures. In some areas he has made remarkable progress. Many diseases have been overcome. The development of medicine and anesthetics greatly reduces pain due to illness and injury. Even the animals share in the benefits!

Man can reduce and prevent certain manifestations of natural evil, but he is not able to banish natural evil altogether. Anesthetic, for example, only numbs us and makes us unable to feel pain; it does not eliminate the condition causing the pain. Furthermore, man's efforts unleash new natural evils. His greed pollutes the environment, although it must be recognized that pollution cannot be entirely avoided in a world with billions of people. And new technological developments such as nuclear energy and atomic weapons are capable of creating even greater natural evils than the earth has ever witnessed. Man is slowly learning what God meant when He said to Adam: "Cursed is the ground because of you" (Genesis 3:17).

CHAPTER TWO

MORAL
EVIL

I

IN the last chapter we saw that some thinkers make too much of natural evil. In response I argued: "It's not as bad as you make out. There isn't as much natural evil as you claim. The picture is already black enough without you making it blacker."

When it comes to moral evil, I find it necessary to take the opposite tack. There is much more moral evil — or sin — than many thinkers are willing to admit. If we are to learn to live with evil, we must take it seriously instead of minimizing or denying it.

Those who claim that they do not see much sin in the world generally operate with a legal or criminal model. They regard sin as *episodic* and assume that the possibility of sin can arise only in certain sorts of circumstances; in other words, certain conditions must be met. The potential sinner must be confronted with two or more alternatives, including at least one which he knows to be good (right) and one which he knows to be bad (wrong). If he freely and knowingly chooses the wrong alternative, he has sinned. Some people prefer to say that he has acted immorally. (For purposes of discussion, I am using the terms *moral evil* and *sin* as virtual synonyms.)

Perhaps you have met people who are not frightened or even uneasy at the prospect of Judgment Day. "If such a thing ever takes place," they assure you, "I'll come out all right. I have nothing on my conscience — or almost nothing."

Such people are working with the legal or criminal or episodic conception of sin. On the basis of such a conception, their claim that they are not sinners makes some sense. Still, although they

17

may lack the self-righteousness of the Pharisees, their conviction that they have done no wrong ultimately places them in the same boat. If they differ from the Pharisees, it is only in that they are not actually expecting to be *rewarded* for their "clean records."

There is much more to sin than such people recognize. In this chapter I will touch on some of the chief points in a Christian understanding of sin. But first I must deal with another mistaken conception of sin.

II

Some people propose a theory of sin and sinfulness that goes too far in the opposite direction. They tell us that there is no escaping the "tragic" dimension in human life. Our sin always clings to us as our fate.

Many who think this way draw inspiration from certain Greek notions. In Sophocles's drama *Oedipus the King* we see this conception of the tragic exemplified. As the protagonist moves toward his fate, it appears that there is nothing to be done about it.

The notion of human life as inherently flawed and tragic has come to expression in various thinkers in the modern world. The most notable of them, perhaps, is Sigmund Freud, who believed that human life is a battle between two opposed, irreconcilable instincts — the instinct for self-preservation (Eros) and the death instinct (Thanatos). Freud writes:

> Starting from speculations on the beginning of life and from biological parallels, I drew the conclusion that, besides the instinct to preserve living substance and to join it into ever larger units, there must exist another, contrary instinct seeking to dissolve those units and to bring them back to their primaeval, inorganic state. That is to say, as well as Eros there was an instinct of death. The phenomenon of life could be explained from the concurrent or mutually opposing action of these two instincts.

> And now, I think, the meaning of the evolution of civilization is no longer obscure to us. It must present the struggle between Eros and Death, between the instinct of life and the instinct of destruction, as it works itself out in the human species. This struggle is what all life essentially consists of, and the evolution of civilization may therefore be simply described as the struggle for life of the human species. And

it is this battle of the giants that our nurse-maids try to appease with their lullaby about Heaven.[1]

From Freud's view one could only conclude that sin is ineradicable. The question then becomes: Will man survive, or will he fall victim to his own destructive instincts?

III

The Calvinist tradition has always taken sin seriously. Calvinists join Freud and various other thinkers in the modern world in affirming that sin is deeply rooted and therefore may not be minimized or explained away.

Is man *depraved* or *deprived*? It is not necessary to choose entirely for the one and entirely against the other. Yet depravity comes closer to expressing what sin is than deprivation.

The notion that sin is a lack and that the sinner is merely deprived has roots deep in the history of the church. Some of the early church fathers engaged in unwarranted speculation about a paradisal "golden age" and the world's alleged "perfection" before the fall into sin. Once Paradise had become something it never was, it seemed only natural to think of sin in terms of deprivation. The comparison between what man possessed *before* the fall and his sorry state *after* the fall suggested that sin is essentially loss.

This conception of sin was not without influence on the Calvinist tradition. Still, leading Calvinist thinkers have realized clearly that sin is a *reality* that we must cope with in life. John Murray writes:

> *Sin is a real evil.* Real in opposition to all theories which regard sin as illusion, and in opposition to all theories that conceive of sin as negation, privation or limitation. Sin is a positive something, . . . not simply the absence of something.
>
> Sin is an event in the spiritual realm of man's mind. Sin originates in the spirit and resides in the spirit. It is not a disturbance in the physical world, not maladjustment to physical conditions. It is a movement in the realm of spirit. But it drastically affects the physical and non-spiritual. Its relationships are cosmic.[2]

We find similar language being used by Louis Berkhof: "It [sin] is not merely something negative, the want of original righteousness, but a positive power of evil."[3]

IV

Those who conceive of sin as episodic, that is, those who understand it in legal or criminal terms, have little idea what to make of the notion of original sin. Most dismiss it outright. And Christian orthodoxy has generally had a hard time explaining what is meant by this doctrine.

Part of the doctrine's meaning is that we who live today share in Adam's guilt; that is to say, we share in the responsibility for the original act of defiance and rebellion against God. Adam, the first sinner, represented us as our covenant head; he was called to choose for all mankind. All of us share in the responsibility for the choice he made.

Is this a strange notion? It will not seem strange if we bear in mind that the Biblical conception of sin and guilt and redemption is thoroughly organic and corporate. Many fell in Adam, and many are raised to new life through the obedience and sacrifice of Christ.

If we stop to think about it, we will see that this corporate emphasis is not so far removed from our experience. Human beings are indeed linked together over the generations by ties that may not be denied. The consciousness of German guilt that lingers on decades after World War II illustrates this point.

When I was a student in Germany, I was fascinated by the question of war guilt. As I watched older men walking down the street, I often wondered what they might have been doing during the years Hitler was in power. Sometimes I had the opportunity to discuss this matter with them. Some of the men insisted that they had simply acted in Germany's best interests, or that they had been forced to act on orders from on high. Others expressed shame and regret.

The question of war guilt also came up in discussions with young Germans. There were a few who said: "I wasn't even born yet when the war ended. All those atrocities of the Hitler era have nothing to do with me!" But many other members of the postwar generation felt a deep shame over what their country and their elders had done. Although they had not participated personally, they carried a burden of guilt anyway and were eager to establish solidarity and friendly ties with people from other countries.

As we think about those young Germans and their feelings of

guilt, we might be inclined to ask ourselves whether they were not taking the question of war guilt a bit too seriously. Can we be responsible for things that happened even before we were born? Yes, in a sense we can. In Adam's sin we sinned too; his guilt is our guilt. Therefore the nineteenth-century mistreatment of the native peoples of North America, for example, may not be dismissed as irrelevant to twentieth-century political issues.

V

The doctrine of original sin also means that sin is somehow "organic" in character. One sin leads to another: sin breeds sin. No sin we commit is wholly without consequences. Herman Bavinck writes:

> Just as in illness the law of sound living continues to operate but is now active in disturbed form, so the organic character of the life of man and of mankind comes to expression in sin. The expression it takes is such that life now develops in a direction diametrically opposed to that which was originally intended. Sin is a slippery plane, and we cannot go along with it a way and then turn around at some arbitrarily selected spot and reverse our course.[4]

Bavinck has provided us with a valuable comparison here: the sinner is a man on a slippery slope. We know how hard it is to move uphill on a sidewalk covered with a sheet of ice; if we move at all, we are more likely to go downhill. That's how it is with the sinner: he slides farther and farther down the hill, with no plateaus along the way.

From this comparison we can see that sin is not simply some act that we "commit" now and then; it is *not* episodic. Man *is* a sinner in a much deeper sense; sin is a web in which he is entangled. His entire life is dominated by his sinfulness. Even his dreams are sinful.

Bavinck's conception of sin is also dynamic, for he speaks of *direction*. The sinner is not rooted to one spot where he sits bemoaning the loss or lack or absence of this or that; no, there is direction in his life. The sinner is *going somewhere*; he is moving away from God.

VI

We cannot talk long about sin without talking about freedom as well. Those who hold the episodic or criminal conception of sin have their difficulties here. If man is *dead* in his trespasses and sins, as the Calvinist tradition maintains, the sinner is surely robbed of all freedom. Is he then an automaton? What could be sinful about an automaton?

Augustine, the great theologian to whom Calvinism traces its roots, already wrestled with this question. He recognized that certain distinctions need to be made regarding sin and freedom.

Man was created free. He was free to live in obedience to God or to rebel against God. He chose the path of rebellion when God confronted him with the test command and told him not to eat of the fruit of a certain tree.

When man "fell" into sin, he became a slave to sin. In a significant sense he was no longer free, for he could no longer avail himself of the pathway of obedience that leads to blessing. Only God's grace could restore him to spiritual life and to fellowship with God.

Natural man or unregenerate man is still on that slippery slope of sin. He simply is not free to move uphill; he is free to go downhill. He may even be able to alter his course slightly to the right or to the left; that is to say, he possesses a certain freedom in choosing between the sins and evils he finds before him on life's downhill pathway.

Conversion, we can now see, is literally a turning around. It presupposes a restoration of man's freedom to follow the uphill path that leads to life and blessing. The new life in Christ makes us free — free to serve (Galatians 5:13).

VII

The question of responsibility is relevant here. How can a person who is dead in trespasses and sins, who is free only to choose between various courses of evil, be held responsible for the sorry, sinful state of affairs in his life? If he "can't help it," do we have any basis for blaming him for his plight?

I believe we do. Once again an example can illustrate that this conception of responsibility is not so far removed from our commonsense way of thinking.

Suppose a man leads a life of too much eating, too much drinking, not enough exercise, and so forth. He continues in this pattern for twenty years, despite various warnings. At age forty his health gives way. He loses his job and can no longer provide for his wife and children. Is he responsible for his plight?

Most people would say that he is. I trust that such a man and his family would be helped, and I don't believe anyone was ever thrown into prison for neglecting his health. Still, the man has something to feel guilty about. In this regard he is in a different situation than a man who cannot provide for his family because he lost his arms and his legs in a freak accident.

Responsibility is often linked with guilt. Nowadays we hear from many quarters that we must do whatever is necessary to get rid of our guilt (and presumably our Calvinism as well). I believe we should resist these appeals. As long as sin is a factor in our lives, guilt will haunt us. If we are to learn to live with evil, we must recognize that there is a place for guilt in human life.

VIII

We sometimes speak of sin as "man's inhumanity to man." *Homo homini lupus* — man is a wolf to man. What man does to his fellow man is indeed frightful, but we will not capture the full reality and meaning of sin if we think only in terms of "horizontal" relationships or person-to-person relationships.

An episode in the life of David can illustrate this for us. David had indeed been a "wolf" to Uriah, one of his faithful soldiers. He took Uriah's wife, and then, to cover up the first sin, he had Uriah murdered, greatly increasing his guilt (see II Samuel 11–12). After David was brought to an awareness of the enormity of his guilt, he poured out his soul before the Lord. What did he say? "I know my transgressions, and my sin is ever before me. Against thee, thee only, have I sinned, and done that which is evil in thy sight" (Psalm 51:3–4).

There is a deep Biblical truth expressed here. In the final analysis, sin must be understood in terms of the relationship between man and God. Horrible as murder is, the increasing distance it brings about between man and God is even more horrible. The sinner turns his back on God and seeks to get ever farther away from God. Sin is transgression, and as such it points always to the One whose law is being trampled underfoot. Sin never stands still, but is constantly moving, with God as the absolute reference point. Herman Bavinck writes:

> Sin is not a substance in itself, but that sort of disturbance of all the gifts and energies given to man which makes them work in another direction, not towards God but away from Him. Reason, will, interests, emotions, passions, psychological and physical abilities of one kind or another — these all were once weapons of righteousness but they have now by the mysterious operation of sin been converted into weapons of unrighteousness.[5]

Sin involves the whole man, who is either actively moving to meet God, that is, moving in His direction, or moving away from Him toward a deification of some creature.

We see, then, that personal — or perhaps existential — categories are more valuable for understanding sin than the legal categories of a system of criminal justice. God does not just cancel our guilt; He adopts us as His sons and daughters. He does not just acquit us by virtue of Christ's all-sufficient sacrifice; He embraces us in His covenant and allows us to call Him Father.

CHAPTER THREE

DEMONIC EVIL

I

FOR many people the word *demon* is synonymous with evil: demons are evil incarnate. But this is not the original meaning. In ancient non-Biblical writings, demons are lesser deities, or sometimes intermediaries between gods and men.

It is helpful to keep this meaning in mind as we consider the use of the word *demon* in modern theological writings. Demons and angels and spirits all amount to roughly the same thing in pre-Christian thought. This may help to explain how the demonic gets linked with the angelic (or even the divine) in so much contemporary thought. The demonic and the angelic are brought together as a dialectical unity of opposites or perhaps as two sides of the same coin.

II

In earlier, more rationalistic times, it was fashionable in intellectual circles to make fun of the very idea of the devil or the demonic. Contemporary thinkers, sobered by two world wars and other horrors of our age, are more inclined to take the notion seriously. Today we encounter a good deal of emphasis on the "reality" of the demonic — or more simply, the reality of the devil.

Now, things are seldom what they seem. We need to be aware that there are people who believe the word *evil* can just as well be spelled with a "d." (Of course there are also people who spell *God* with two "o's.") On the very first page of Ruth Nanda Anshen's book entitled *The Reality of the Devil* we read: "Although

I am attempting to deal with the reality of the Devil, this is only
another way of saying that the Devil is in man — man who takes
leave of his senses and falls prey to his own passions, to vice,
selfishness, falsehood, vanity, lust, greed, superstition, fanaticism."[1] The book's subtitle is: "Evil in Man." Anshen does not
mean to deny outright that the devil exists; what she proposes to
do is to deal with evil in human life. Who would wish to deny
that man is evil?

One of the theologians of our time who has made much of "the
demonic" is Paul Tillich. He uses the term in ways that do not
seem to fit in with traditional Christian thought. What does he
mean by it? In a book on Tillich by James Luther Adams we read:

> The demonic is not a tangible entity. Like the terms "unconditioned,"
> "ground," "abyss," "divine," it is not something that can be identified
> unambiguously. All of these terms refer to aspects, to qualities of
> existence. Hence the demonic is an aspect, a power, in the structure
> of existence.[2]

It is sometimes suggested that Hitler was a manifestation of
the demonic. Or perhaps an oppressive state could be characterized
as demonic. So enormous and horrible is the evil perpetrated in
the name of the state in our century that the desire to brand
totalitarian and oppressive regimes as demonic is fully understandable.

III

John Hick is one of the thinkers who have difficulty making up
their minds about the existence of Satan. Does a doctrine of Satan
help us solve the problem of evil? Hick writes:

> It will be noticed that I have not thus far mentioned Satan and the
> satanic kingdom. . . . By this omission I do not intend to deny the
> existence of energies and structures of evil transcending individual
> human minds, but to indicate that any such forces are part of the
> general problem of evil, logically co-ordinate with human wickedness,
> and do not constitute a unique kind of evil that might provide a key
> to the solution of the problem as a whole. The puzzles attending
> human imperfection, free will, and sin are reiterated, but not further
> illumined, by transferring them to a superhuman plane.[3]

There is something to what Hick says: the doctrine of Satan does not clear up the mystery about the origin of evil. But we should not draw the wrong conclusion and declare that the doctrine of Satan is of no importance. Herman Bavinck, for one, insists that this doctrine is by no means insignificant in relation to Christian doctrine as a whole.[4]

What happens if we do not have a Biblical doctrine of Satan? Given the oppressive presence of evil in our world, we then wind up talking about "the demonic" as incarnated in leaders like Hitler and in the totalitarian state.

To take this step is somehow to isolate and separate evil: we make evil so concrete and specific that we can literally point to it. Ironically enough, Hitler did exactly that when he made the Jews the incarnation of evil, and many communists do the same when they equate evil with the capitalists or the rich. Those who think along such lines find it all too easy to decide what to do with these incarnations of evil: they must be either liquidated or, if that should not prove feasible, "reeducated" (i.e., brainwashed).

In Christian circles a comparable error is sometimes made. Once evil or the demonic is identified with certain political or governmental structures and leaders, the next step is to identify God and goodness with those who take it upon themselves to combat oppressive structures and people. Thus we sometimes hear that God (or Jesus) is "in" politics. What is meant, apparently, is that He somehow acts as a participant in the political struggles of our time, and is perhaps incarnate in certain political movements and forces. Ronald Sider, for example, talks about a "biblical teaching that God is on the side of the poor."[5] The appeal to "identify" with the poor is based on more than just sympathy. Christians, we are sometimes told, are obligated to side with the liberation movements abroad and the political groups in our own land that are fighting discrimination, sexism, racism, and so forth.

I'm afraid this way of thinking has dangerous consequences. Once we identify our political opponents as incarnations of evil or "the demonic" and become convinced that God is on our side, we can easily fall prey to the politics of fanaticism and lose our ability to look critically at our own strategies and actions. The Calvinist tradition has by no means been free from guilt in this area, but in its conception of politics it has at least tried to avoid the mistake of incarnating God in human political movements.

The key to this question is the relation between God and the political process. If we erase the boundary between Creator and creature and make God an agent among other agents in the historical stream of events, we can hardly avoid the conclusion that He is on this side or that. Therefore the Calvinist tradition emphasizes that God relates to the political process primarily through the creation order and through the political and governmental structures that are called into being in response to it. If those structures are faithful to the demands of the creation order, we can affirm that they are doing God's will in politics; yet we still have a basis for judging and criticizing, for we have *not* identified any human leaders and structures active in history with God Himself. If Jesus is indeed "in" this or that liberation movement, how would we ever dare whisper a word of criticism?

Such are the dangers involved in identifying evil as "the demonic." Aleksandr Solzhenitsyn has issued a timely warning against the tendency to locate evil in others, in our enemies: "If only there were evil people somewhere insidiously committing evil deeds, and it were necessary only to separate them from the rest of us and destroy them. But the line dividing good and evil cuts through the heart of every human being."[6]

IV

Bavinck is right: the doctrine of Satan is no minor matter. Yet, though it is important for us to know who Satan is, it remains extremely difficult to make responsible and detailed theological statements about him. Bavinck speaks of the "incomprehensibility" of the fallen angels and observes: "Because of this incomprehensibility of the devils, many have denied their existence, or regarded them as the souls of the dead or as personifications of our wicked sins or as impersonal principles of evil. But Scripture places the reality of Satan and his angels beyond doubt. . . ."[7]

The Bible talks specifically about demons in a number of passages, and therefore we need not be altogether silent on the subject. Perhaps the main point to be made — especially in the face of the Manichaean threat to the Christian outlook — is that the demons are creatures; they are angels of God. They fell into sin some time before man fell, which means that the origin of sin is actually found before the episode in the garden of Eden. Satan tempted man to sin — but only after God confronted man with the choice between good and evil, the choice between life and death.

Since the demons are creatures, they are not absolutely evil. Nothing created by God is wholly without goodness. For this reason, too, it is wrong to identify "the demonic" as the focus and concentration point of all evil.

V

One of the most fundamental misconceptions about Satan is that he urges man to pursue evil rather than good. Under the influence of Manichaeism, we still tend to think of God and Satan as complete opposites. This is a misunderstanding. The issue in the struggle between God and Satan is what — or who — is to define the good.

We must not make the mistake of regarding good as somehow more ultimate than God. The good is rooted in God's sovereign will as Creator. In a simply written book about Satan and the occult, J. Stafford Wright declares: "The essence of *good* and *bad* in the Bible is harmony or lack of harmony with God. If we do not understand this, we run into difficulties over how a good God could create bad beings. There will always be a mystery about evil, but essentially evil is saying no to God."[8]

If man is to say no to God, he must have something better to cling to instead. Only when we recognize this do we see what Satan was up to in tempting Adam and Eve. Denis de Rougemont writes:

> It is not evil in itself which tempts, but always a good which one imagines, an even better good than that which God offers. . . . Eve was not tempted by an evil thing, but by a very fine and good apple, pleasant to the eyes and precious to the Spirit. She was not tempted by the desire to harm, but by the idea of achieving divinity.[9]

It was never Satan's intention, then, to sell man on the delights of evil. What he did instead was to preach a false gospel, a perverted account of where the good is to be sought. Arthur Pink observed earlier in this century:

> Satan is the arch-counterfeiter. As we have seen, the Devil is now busy at work in the same field in which the Lord sowed the good seed. He is seeking to prevent the growth of the wheat by another plant

— the tares, which closely resemble the wheat in appearance. In a word, by a process of *imitation* he is aiming to neutralise the Work of Christ. Therefore, as Christ has a Gospel, Satan has a gospel, too; the latter being a clever counterfeit of the former. So closely does the gospel of Satan resemble that which it parodies, multitudes of the unsaved are deceived by it.

The *apostles* of Satan are not saloon-keepers and white-slave traffikers, but are for the most part ordained ministers. Thousands of those who occupy our modern pulpits are no longer engaged in presenting the fundamentals of the Christian Faith, but have turned aside from the Truth and have given heed to fables. Instead of magnifying the enormity of sin and setting forth its eternal consequences, they minimise it by declaring that sin is merely ignorance or the absence of good.[10]

What is the content of Satan's gospel? Does he demand that people worship him? Or does he suggest that people should worship themselves and glorify all their own impulses?

There are many people in North America today who worship Satan by name; some of them engage in absurd and disgusting rituals. But other Satan worshipers are essentially believers in the false gospel he preaches and are not much concerned with the question whether there really and truly is a fallen angel named Satan. Anton LaVey, a self-proclaimed "high priest" of Satan, explains that the gospel of Satan is in essence the message of Humanism:

> The Satanist is the ultimate humanist. The Satanist realizes that man can be his own worst enemy and must often be protected against himself. The average man sets up situations for himself so he can be a loser. We Satanists have ancient rituals which exorcise those needs for self-abasement before they happen.
>
> The Satanic principle is that man willfully controls his destiny; if he doesn't, some other man — a lot smarter than he is — will.
>
> Satanically speaking, anarchy and chaos must ensue for awhile before a new Satanic morality can prevail. The new Satanic morality won't be very different from the old law of the jungle wherein right and wrong were judged in the truest natural sense of biting and being bitten back.[11]

VI

We should not conclude, however, that the activities of Satan are manifested only in the false ideas and utter perversion of morality that we see all around us today. Satan works in other ways as well. In the New Testament era demons often took "possession" of human beings, and the gospels record several stories about demons being cast out by Christ and His apostles.

Phenomena strikingly parallel to demon possession are still reported in many parts of the world today. We read, for example, accounts of exorcisms, usually conducted by priests of the Roman Catholic Church. Some scholars believe there has been no demon possession since the age of the apostles, although many contemporary phenomena would seem to suggest that such scholars are wrong.

Admittedly, the notion of demon possession has been sensationalized and exploited in recent years. Most of the popular movies and fictionalized accounts are of little or no theological or spiritual value, and some are in decidedly bad taste. Still, even if much of the literature concerning demon possession and exorcism is in fact nonsense, we need not conclude that there is no such thing as demon possession.

Witchcraft is another phenomenon often associated with demonic activity. Once again, much nonsense has been written. Yet it cannot be denied that there have been — and still are — people who call themselves witches and who claim to engage in mysterious rituals. Are we to take such claims seriously?

Jeffrey Burton Russell, a historian who has undertaken a careful study of witchcraft, writes:

> The question "Do you really believe in witchcraft?" usually means to inquire whether one subscribes to every folly that fiction and fancy have assigned to witches, and one is obliged to answer no. On the other hand if one places witchcraft in the context of the worldwide phenomenon of demon worship and witch belief, one will answer differently. As Arago observed, "Outside of pure mathematics, anyone who pronounces the word 'impossible' is lacking in prudence."[12]

Sober words indeed. The Bible's condemnation of sorcery and witchcraft should also give us something to think about, suggesting as it does the existence of magicians and witches who wield some sort of supernatural power.

If demonic forces do indeed lie behind some of the witchcraft in our world, it does not appear that the sole intent of such forces is to cause destruction and harm. Rather, the apparent demonic strategy is to mislead people and keep them from worshiping the God who reveals Himself in Scripture as the maker of the heavens and the earth. People who come into possession of a power not available to others will probably be willing to give the worship of their hearts to that power — or perhaps to the source of that power. Witchcraft, in short, is not to be taken lightly.

VII

Our theme is learning to live with evil. One of the things required of us is that we take evil seriously and develop a respect (if that is not too positive a term) for its power. Therefore we must also take demonic evil seriously. A healthy fear is in order.

Martin Luther certainly reckoned with the possibility of demonic evil. Indeed, some say he went too far in ascribing evil of every sort to demons. John Calvin, on the other hand, advised caution in identifying demons as the cause of this world's woes. The theologian Charles Hodge sides with Calvin on this score:

> We are not to deny what are plainly recorded in the Scriptures as facts on this subject; we have no right to assert that Satan and his angels do not now in any cases produce similar effects; but we should abstain from asserting the fact of Satanic or demoniacal influence or possession in any case where the phenomena can be otherwise accounted for. [13]

The Calvinist tradition has been cautious, then, in what it has affirmed concerning the activities of angels and demons. Hence Herman Bavinck observes that the Protestant confessions do not have much to say on the subject of angels. If the Calvinists have erred, he believes, it is on the side of saying too little rather than too much. [14]

Bavinck, writing many years ago, may well have been justified in making this comment, but it is also possible to err in the other direction. In a recent book on Satan we read a warning against the contemporary preoccupation with the devil: "Contemporary thought is wrong not because, as was the case ten or fifteen years ago, it makes too little of Satan. It is wrong because it makes too much of him. Contemporary thought presents him as if he, not Jesus, is the superior one." [15]

We see, then, that it is not easy to present a balanced and Scripturally complete view of Satan without going too far in one direction or the other. Hendrikus Berkhof sums up the main motifs in the Christian belief in angels and demons:

> The accounts of angels are based on a threefold assumption which is certainly closely related to the Israelite-Christian faith. The appearances of angels give expression to the belief that (a) God's world, including those beings who are consciously subject to him, is far richer than what can be seen on our planet; (b) outside this provisional and alienated world there are other realities which already now are fully and perfectly filled with his glory; and (c) those worlds do not look down with contempt on our darkened planet but possess a genuine willingness to be used in the service of God's love for man to help our world reach its destination.[16]

Many people in the world today are convinced there is nothing more to reality than what our senses allow us to perceive. Therefore we need a Christian doctrine of angels and demons to remind ourselves and others that things are not quite as simple as certain rationalists would have us believe.

PART TWO

CONCEPTIONS OF EVIL

INTELLECTUAL problems are sometimes oversimplified. People like to argue: "If you reject position A, you'll have to accept position B. You must choose between A and B — it's as simple as that."

I suspect that in most cases such a choice is not quite so simple. A number of theories, for example, attempt to account for the problem of evil. Yet we are sometimes told that one must choose between the Manichaean view, which awards evil definite ontological status, that is, makes it something real, and the deprivation theory, usually associated with the Platonist tradition, which denies ontological status to evil.

Although there are in fact more choices than these two alternatives, the Manichaean view (Chapter 4) is indeed a good place to start. Manichaeism is the position which most theories of evil either echo or react against. The thinkers who view evil as necessary (Chapter 5) bear some resemblance to the Manichaeans, although with certain definite differences which should not be overlooked. The Platonist tradition, with its theory of evil as deprivation or non-being (Chapter 6), clearly represents a wholesale rejection of Manichaeism. Those who think along the lines of Augustine and Calvin (Chapter 7) hold yet another view, but they, too, are eager to dispose of Manichaeism as incompatible with a worthy conception of God.

The view of evil which I shall defend fits within the Augustinian tradition. Yet I do not mean to attribute my formulation of it to either Augustine or Calvin. Hence, in a separate chapter with which Part II concludes, I will spell out my own view, making in the process a special effort to clarify the relations between natural evil, moral evil, and demonic evil.

CHAPTER FOUR

EVIL
AS ULTIMATE:
MANICHAEISM

I

MANICHAEISM developed in the days of the Roman empire — about two centuries after Christ. It was a time of many bizarre competing religions. Scholars have a hard time determining the relationships of the various religions and cults to one another. Some are simply variants on a common theme, but certain of them are indeed original.

Manichaeism is not fully distinguishable from Gnosticism. In fact, the former can best be understood if we first have some knowledge of the latter. Mani, the founder of Manichaeism, has even been called "the last of the great Gnostics."[1]

"Gnosticism" has a more contemporary ring to it than "Manichaeism." Various recent scholars have pointed out that Gnosticism is still influential in our time, even if some of the people under its influence don't know what the word means. "Manichaeism," on the other hand, sounds antiquated.

Gnosticism is a mixture of ideas from various quarters. One of its central elements is a doctrine of salvation, an account of what man must do to be saved from the evils of this life. Those evils are the "lower" things — matter and the body. Salvation represents an escape from the body to the "higher" things. And the key to the escape is a special sort of knowledge (Greek *gnosis*). Naturally, this doctrine could also be developed in a mystical direction. Classical mysticism is concerned not just with feeling but also with knowledge or a "seeing" of the mind.

II

Gnosticism overlaps somewhat with Manichaeism, for the latter offers a similar doctrine of salvation. Both conceive of knowledge as central. One of the major differences between the two, however, is that Manichaeism involves a more extensive metaphysics or interpretation of reality. In fact, Manichaeism is today chiefly known for its metaphysics, its unique understanding of the relation between good and evil as forces or principles which actually exist.

Manichaeism developed in Persia, where the Zoroastrian religious tradition offered a dualistic conception of good and evil as ultimate principles. Mani seems to have adopted this basic dualism and combined it with ideas from many different sources. The result was a new religious synthesis that testified to considerable ingenuity and breadth of vision on the part of its creator.

Manichaeism flatly rejects the idea that evil has a beginning. There was no fall from a state of goodness. Evil is something real that did not come into being after goodness but always coexisted with it. In his metaphysics or theory of reality, Mani places good and evil, light and darkness, spirit and matter over against each other as opposites that will never be unified or reconciled.

In most discussions of the problem of evil, any view that grants some reality to evil is referred to as "dualistic." It is questionable whether the use of this term is wise: it could well be argued that a genuine dualism calls for two principles that are completely equal in status. Even in the case of Manichaeism it has been questioned whether evil and darkness enjoy a status fully equivalent to that of goodness. Some scholars therefore have reservations about characterizing Manichaeism as "dualism."[2]

III

To further our aim of learning to live with evil, we must examine the practical consequences of the Manichaean conception of evil.

Strictly speaking, the Manichaeans had no intention of living with evil or putting up with it. In their view, evil is ultimate; therefore it is neither to be destroyed nor redeemed. Since evil must be regarded as a potent force, the best thing to do is to avoid it as much as possible — or flee it altogether.

To do so calls for an ethic of asceticism or self-denial. Death is man's ultimate deliverance: it releases the soul from the realm of matter and darkness. The body, according to this view, is a prison.

Until death comes, an ascetic way of life is the most prudent course to follow. The Manichaeans did not make their strict demands on everyone; they had a category of second-class members of their fellowship for whom more latitude was allowed. (Augustine was a "second-class" Manichaean in his early years.) For those belonging to the inner circle, however, there was no place for sexual relations. Food, of course, could not be avoided altogether; still, meat (or anything "ensouled") was ruled out. Wine was also forbidden.

To people living today, Manichaeism seems a distant, almost unreal phenomenon. We can understand what an ascetic lifestyle might involve, but that bizarre theory of reality as a mixture of good and bad, light and darkness, is foreign to the contemporary mind. Yet Manichaeism was an outlook with definite consequences for practical, day-to-day affairs. Peter Brown tells us how the Manichaean thought of himself:

> He could identify himself only with a part of himself, his "good soul". So much of him plainly did not belong to this oasis of purity: the tensions of his own passions, his rage, his sexuality, his corrupt body, the vast, pullulating world of "nature red in tooth and claw" outside him. All this weighed upon him. It was obvious that what was good in him wished to be "set free", to "return", to merge again into an untroubled, original state of perfection — a "Kingdom of Light" — from which it felt isolated. Yet is was equally plain that men had failed to carry out this, the only possible desire of their better nature.

> The Manichees were austere men. They were recognizable, at the time, by their pale faces; and, in modern literature, they have been presented as the purveyors of the bleakest pessimism. Yet they reserved this pessimism for only one side of themselves. They regarded the other side, their "mind", their "good soul", as quite untarnished: it was, quite literally, a crumb of the divine substance. Their religion was directed to ensuring that this, the good part of themselves, would remain essentially untouched and unaffected by their baser nature.[3]

IV

Although it has not been established beyond dispute that Manichaeism represents dualism in the strict sense, the term *dualism* is regularly applied to other thinkers who somehow "separate" good and evil as two different spheres or principles. One such thinker is Marcion, who lived during the second century and is also associated with Gnosticism.

Marcion's "dualism" is his fundamental contrast between Law and Grace. Whenever such a contrast is drawn, there is a tendency to associate one of the pair of opposites with evil, and the other with good. In Marcion's case, it is clear that Law is evil and Grace is good.

Although there are various resemblances between Mani and Marcion, the "dualism" of the latter is not to be understood in metaphysical terms. E. C. Blackman writes:

> Marcion saw two principles at work in the universe. The first is the principle of Justice or Law, inherent in the universe and in fact the originator of it; not entirely regardless of man, but responsible for "Nature red in tooth and claw"; responsible for human nature as well, particularly for the sense of obligation which causes man to see certain actions as duties without supplying always the power to perform them. The second principle intervenes and overrules Justice; we may call it Grace or Redeeming Love. Man can come under the dominion of this second principle and then he is delivered from the bondage of the first.[4]

Salvation is thus essentially a movement toward one principle and away from the other.

Although Marcion eventually became the founder of a movement of his own, much of his work was carried on in a Christian setting. He has had considerable influence on the Christian church, and his ideas are by no means dead today; in fact, they sound downright familiar. Blackman writes:

> He thought Christianity could be understood without reference to anything that happened before A.D. 29; the content of the Gospel could be accounted for from within the circle of the Church as it had developed since that date. To this the answer is that he was wrong. The teaching of Christ and its impact on Judaism is not explicable without reference to the history of Judaism.[5]

We are here moving in a direction that could be called "doubting the Old Testament." Some Christian thinkers are so impressed with the doctrine of God's grace in the New Testament that they simply equate goodness with the "God of love." Marcion drew the conclusion that suggested itself: the Old Testament is not to be regarded as Scripture. In fact, he could not find the New Testament "God of love" in the Old Testament at all. Instead he found a stern Creator whose chief attribute was justice.

By the time Marcion was done, his Bible consisted of no more

than ten letters of Paul and an expurgated Gospel of Luke. The
Old Testament's Judaistic influence was so strong in the other New
Testament books that Marcion felt he had to reject them.

V

As we move to more recent thinkers, we find that the charge of
"dualism" is also raised against Martin Luther. Luther certainly
did not embrace Mani's metaphysics, nor did he fall into Marcion's
trap by removing justice from God's nature. Luther was well acquainted with the God of the Scriptures as a God of wrath, a God
who punishes. Still, he is sometimes called a "dualist."

In Luther we find a contrast between Law and Gospel, between
the original order of creation and the spiritual Kingdom of Christ.
Although these two cannot simply be correlated with evil and
good respectively, Luther did tend to play off the temporal order
against the spiritual order. H. Richard Niebuhr observes:

> For Luther the wrath of God is manifested not only against sin, but
> against the whole temporal world. Hence there is . . . not only a
> yearning for the new life in Christ through the death of the self to
> itself, but also a desire for the death of the body and for the passing
> of the temporal order.

> There seems to be a tendency in dualism, as represented by . . . Lu-
> ther, to relate temporality or finiteness to sin in such a degree as to
> move creation and fall into very close proximity, and in that connec-
> tion to do less than justice to the creative work of God.[6]

Such an outlook, of course, has consequences for daily life.
How does the Lutheran Christian learn to live with evil? At this
point the theme of asceticism comes up again: self-denial is called
for.

We also find an ascetic emphasis in Calvinism. Here we seem
to have agreement between the two major Protestant traditions.
Yet the Calvinist call for discipline, sobriety, and dedication cannot
be equated with the Lutheran brand of asceticism. Ernst Troeltsch
observes:

> Within this sphere of general agreement, however, Lutheranism and
> Calvinism developed along very different lines. They divided between
> them the two fundamentally different aspects of asceticism which have
> already been mentioned: the spirit of metaphysical depreciation of this

sinful world [Lutheranism], and the systematic discipline of the senses [Calvinism]. Lutheranism depreciated this world, mourning over it as a "vale of tears", but so far as everything else was concerned the Lutheran, happy in the assurance of justification, and nourished by the Presence of Christ in the sacraments, let things remain as they were, quite happy and confident, accepting the world as he found it, exhibiting Christian love in faithfulness to the duties of his calling, leaving results to God, and incidentally thankfully rejoicing in the Divine glory of creation which breaks through the shadows cast by this sinful world.[7]

Lutheranism, then, regards this world as a "vale of tears." Still, it accepts evil in society and nature, for the world's destiny is in God's hand. It has often been asked whether the prevalence of this outlook in the Protestant churches of Germany did not account for their relative acquiescence during Hitler's rise to power. Given the Lutheran framework, how could one expect anything good from the state, which is, after all, part of the temporal order? The wrath of God rests upon the entire temporal order — including both the Nazi state and its political enemies.

CHAPTER FIVE

EVIL AS NECESSARY: HEGEL AND SCHLEIERMACHER

I

OUR topic in Part II is conceptions of evil or theories of evil. In the previous chapter we looked at the theory that evil is "ultimate," that is, an ineradicable part of reality. Evil, according to such a view, is to be fled rather than combated or destroyed.

In this chapter we will look at some thinkers who maintain that evil is "necessary." This position somewhat resembles the view that evil is "ultimate," but with a very significant difference: it holds that good can only be (or become) what it is through some sort of association or struggle with evil. The theory we are offered, then, is that evil is necessary in order that there be goodness.

This view of evil has numerous defenders in our time — many more than I could deal with in this chapter. A representative spokesman is Duncan Littlefair, who argues: "The more we learn about good, the more we learn about evil, for evil is part of the good, wherever it is found. I believe we will never be able to separate one clearly from the other." The "God versus Satan" myth may no longer be adequate or satisfactory for expressing the relationship between good and evil. Littlefair speaks instead of "the importance of the animal in us." There is a sense in which we *need* evil, according to Littlefair: "The only way to enhance the good in our lives is to see the evil."[1]

II

Two of the most important proponents of the view that evil is somehow necessary are G. W. F. Hegel and F. D. E. Schleiermacher, who both taught at the University of Berlin early in the nineteenth century. The former was a philosopher and the latter a theologian. As so often happens when great men work in close proximity, they did not get along well together. Each developed a unique, original way of thinking independent of the other; yet each came to the conclusion that evil is necessary for the sake of the good.

Hegel is one of the most controversial philosophers of all time. He has been extensively criticized and ridiculed. Sidney Hook complains that Hegel's philosophy "vulgarizes tragedy" as it tries to convince man that ". . . his agony and defeat are not really evils but necessary elements in the goodness of the whole."[2]

Hegel also has his defenders. In fact, many philosophers who do not share his overall viewpoint admire his "idealism" because they see in it a sober "realism." Hegel's philosophy does not flee or ignore the harsh realities of evil; it tries to comprehend them and place them in a larger framework in which they take on some meaning.

Hegel's key insight with regard to evil is that although it is necessary, it is only provisional. He uses cumbersome language to make his philosophical points, but in the end he manages to erase the boundary between the finite mind of man and the infinite mind of God. His conception of the relation between the finite and the infinite results in a unique characterization of evil: it is undeniably real, but eventually absorbed into a larger whole which can only be called good.

This enterprise led Hegel in the direction of theodicy, that is, a justification of God's goodness in the face of all the evil in the world. Leibniz had formulated the classic theodicy when he argued that God must have surveyed all the possible worlds and created the best of them. This, of course, was a starkly logical, abstract response to the problem of evil. Hegel's theodicy, by contrast, was historical in character: he suggested that the existence of evil could be understood in the light of the full sweep of world history. James Collins examines the contrast between Leibniz's theodicy and Hegel's interpretation of God as absolute spirit:

> Leibniz ultimately failed because he kept the being of God distinct from the historical process, from the finitude, evil, and error in history. Hegel's absolute spirit does not merely hover over history and finite frailty; it lives and develops by means of them.

Full justification belongs only to the historical process as a whole, and in this judgment a perfect reconciliation is made with all the defects, errors, and evils of our historical experience. . . . In Hegel's hands, the older theodicy is converted into philosophy of history because the latter definitively replaces the opposition between God and moral evil by a totality, within which evil is a justified episode in the temporal evolution of the absolute.[3]

When we turn from the language of philosophy of history to the language of theology and Scripture, we see that new meanings are needed for old doctrines and phrases. Every man is Adam; that is to say, every man falls — and has fallen, into sin. Adam is by nature both good and evil. E. L. Fackenheim formulates Hegel's position as follows:

> Christian faith thus sees man as in a paradoxical condition. He is by nature good. For he is created in the image of God apart from his own doing, and his knowledge of being so created (which is the original human act) is for that reason also the original anti-divine act. But he is also, and at the same time, by nature evil, for the divine image remains potential until he himself rises to the knowledge which actualizes it. Hence animal innocence is an imaginary past always already lost, and the guilt which is man's self-willed condition is also his God-willed destiny.[4]

In this manner orthodox Christian doctrine undergoes a complete reinterpretation by Hegel. His ability to link his own philosophical ideas with traditional Christian terms and symbols is part of the reason for his enormous impact on theology.

III

The Hegelian approach to the problems of theology and the problem of God and evil has been much imitated. Some of the imitators follow Hegel more in style than in substance. This can be said especially of the thinkers who argue that God is finite and is doing His (limited) best to restrain and overcome evil. Such arguments may sound Hegelian, but the basic position is actually some distance removed from Hegel's thought.

One of the leading representatives of this point of view is Edgar S. Brightman, who makes a definitely un-Hegelian distinction between God and "the Given." That which is outside God includes what Brightman calls "surd evil," that is, "a type of evil which is inherently and irreducibly evil and contains within itself no principle of development or improvement." As an example he points to imbecility or feeble-mindedness: "Let us grant that imbecility may encourage psychiatry and arouse pity; yet, if it be an incurable condition, there remains in it a surd evil embodied in the intrinsic worthlessness of the imbecile's existence and the suffering which his existence imposes upon others."[5]

S. Paul Schilling, who defends a similar view, speaks of "purposeless evil" and suggests that there may be "internal boundaries in the power of God."[6] God is like man in that He must choose the course of action that causes the least harm.

Strictly speaking, such views of evil have more affinity with Manichaeism than with Hegel's thought, for they present evil as ineradicable and unavoidable — in short, as ultimate. We also see the essential affinity with Manichaeism when we contrast the overall lack of hope in such thinkers as Brightman and Schilling with the cosmic optimism of Hegel.

IV

In the figure of Schleiermacher we encounter a thinker who surely rivals Hegel in importance and influence. Schleiermacher represents the beginning of a new era in theology, an era in which the notion of God as the object of theology underwent a fateful transformation. Like Hegel, Schleiermacher brought man and God together in such a way that it became necessary to talk about man in talking about God.

The key to Schleiermacher's conception of evil is that man's original goodness and his sinfulness are not temporally separated in history. Traditional Christian theology had spoken of man as having been created good by God and later falling into a state of continuing sinfulness. For Schleiermacher, however, righteousness and sin are two original dispositions of the soul. Therefore sin breaks into human life not just at the time of Adam's fall but at every moment in history. Richard R. Niebuhr writes: "Religion, sin and blessedness are not three wholly different phenomena. They are not external to each other; each is a part in the others, each names the whole of which the others are parts."[7]

What we find in Schleiermacher's thought is a reversal of perspective. If we are to seek a pristine goodness of man, we must look for it not in some original state of perfection but in what man is headed for. When we speak of man's goodness, we are not talking the language of creation but the language of eschatology or the future.

If we keep an eye fixed on the process of redemption that is underway, we can see in what sense evil is "necessary" for Schleiermacher. God uses sin to drive man into His arms. C. W. Christian explains Schleiermacher's position as follows:

> Insofar as sin is real, and insofar as all things owe their existence to God, sin must have its source in God. In a system that affirms both God's sovereignty and his goodness, there is no way to avoid tracing evil and sin back to the author of the system. . . . Yet we cannot regard him as the author of sin in the same sense that he is the author of redemption. Sin can be instrumental but not ultimate. It corresponds positively to no attribute of God. The presence of sin and grace together in the Christian consciousness points to the fact that ultimately sin exists that it might be overcome by reconciliation.[8]

One of the strengths of Schleiermacher's perspective is its comprehensiveness. He does not leave natural evil out of the picture but tells us that it is rooted in sin (moral evil) and can only be overcome when the latter is wiped away by God's universal salvation.

V

There is a definite theodicy implied in Schleiermacher's thought. John Hick, a contemporary thinker, has stated it ably, acknowledging his indebtedness to Schleiermacher and also to Irenaeus, a second-century thinker, and Tatian, a forerunner of Irenaeus. According to Hick, Tatian maintained that "God did not make men already good, but made them free to become good by obedience to Himself."[9]

Sin is "virtually inevitable" in this view. Hick assigns it an "instrumental" character; it is needed in order for the good to come into being.[10] (We already encountered this conception of sin as "instrumental" in connection with Schleiermacher.)

Borrowing a phrase from a letter of the poet John Keats, Hick characterizes this world with its many evils as a "vale of soul-making,"[11] as opposed to a "vale of tears." It may be the latter as well, but Hick maintains that we can best cope with evil by viewing it as the former.

Such a theodicy does call for some theological renovation. Hick writes: "Because we can no longer share the assumption, upon which traditional Christian theodicy has been built, that the creation-fall myth is basically authentic history, we inevitably look at that theodicy critically and see in it inadequacies to which in the past piety has tended to blind the eyes of faith."[12] What is wrong with the traditional view of evil, which Hick associates with Augustine? A number of things:

> This theory, so simple and mythologically satisfying, is open to insuperable scientific, moral, and logical objections. To begin with less fundamental aspects of the traditional solution, we know today that the conditions that were to cause human disease and mortality and the necessity for man to undertake the perils of hunting and the labours of agriculture and building, were already part of the natural order prior to the emergence of man and prior therefore to any first human sin, as were also the conditions causing such further "evils" as earthquake, storm, flood, drought, and pest. And, second, the policy of punishing the whole succeeding human race for the sin of just the first pair is, by the best human moral standards, unjust and does not provide anything that can be recognized by these standards as a theodicy. Third, there is a basic and fatal incoherence at the heart of the mythically based "solution". The Creator is preserved from any responsibility for the existence of evil by the claim that He made men (or angels) as free and finitely perfect creatures, happy in the knowledge of Himself, and subject to no strains or temptations, but that they themselves inexplicably and inexcusably rebelled against Him. But this suggestion amounts to a sheer self-contradiction. It is impossible to conceive of wholly good beings in a wholly good world becoming sinful.[13]

What this quotation shows us, among other things, is that the problem of evil is by no means peripheral to Christian theology: a decision with regard to evil will have consequences for many other doctrines. Hick is aware of this. Having rejected the account of man's origins presented in the Bible, he offers in its place a "two-stage" conception of the creation of man. The first stage was the creation of man as a creature for whom fellowship with God is a possibility. We are now in the second stage. Writes Hick: "Men may eventually become the perfected persons whom the

New Testament calls 'children of God', but they cannot be created ready-made as this."[14]

If the "traditional" view of evil is to be upheld in the face of the criticism of Hick and other such thinkers, special attention will have to be given to two questions. First, in what sense — if any — was there evil in the world before man was created? Second, can we offer any response to the charge that God is unjust? In other words, do generally accepted human standards of goodness and justice enable us to determine what sort of being God can and cannot be?

EVIL AS NON-BEING: THE PLATONIST TRADITION

I

THE categories of pessimism and optimism are sometimes useful in discussing evil. Those who view evil as ultimate (Chapter 4) can be regarded as *pessimists* in that they do not believe that evil will ever go away or be harmonized with good or be taken up into a larger picture that could be called good. Those who view evil as necessary (Chapter 5) might be thought of as *realists*. They take evil seriously, but end up neither pessimists nor optimists with regard to man's plight in the present. They maintain that evil must always be reckoned with, although there is the possibility — indeed, likelihood — of its somehow being made subservient to purposes of good.

There are a great many thinkers who, in one way or another, arrive at the conclusion that evil is not real. Evil, they tell us, is illusory; it is non-being. If this is the case, human beings ought to be *optimists*, which is just what most thinkers of this persuasion are.

One of the most eloquent spokesmen for this position is Ralph Waldo Emerson. In his essay on self-reliance, he expresses his optimism as follows:

> Discontent is the want of self-reliance: it is infirmity of will. Regret calamities, if you can thereby help the sufferer; if not, attend your own work, and already the evil begins to be repaired. Our sympathy is just as base. We come to them who weep foolishly, and sit down and cry for company, instead of imparting to them truth and health in rough electric shocks, putting them once more in communication with their own reason.[1]

Given such an outlook, we do not find much of a conception

of tragedy in Emerson. In his essay "The Tragic," we read: "Frankly then it is necessary to say that all sorrow dwells in a low region. It is superficial; for the most part fantastic, or in the appearance and not in things. Tragedy is in the eye of the observer, and not in the heart of the sufferer."[2]

These are not statements Emerson makes lightly. They are rooted in a metaphysical system, a philosophy that attempts to explain the nature of good and evil. Elsewhere Emerson writes: "Good is positive. Evil is merely privative, not absolute: it is like cold, which is the privation of heat. All evil is so much death or nonentity."[3]

II

The key word in Emerson's view of evil is *privation*. Not many thinkers or writers claim to have a "solution" to the problem of evil. Of the few who do, most tell us that evil is a privation, a lack.

Roman Catholic authors sometimes maintain that the solution is to be found in the writings of Thomas Aquinas, who, in turn, borrowed heavily from Aristotle, who maintained that evil is privation of being. François Petit claims that Aquinas "step by step solves the enigma of evil." Christians therefore have some basis for optimism. Petit writes: "A provisional, but valid and complete, solution to this problem [of evil] can be given by repeating the words sung by the deacon in the Easter Vigil: *O felix culpa . . .*" ("O happy fault, to win for us so great and mighty a Redeemer!").[4] Despite the fall into sin, we wind up better off than ever in the end.

The analysis of evil in Thomas Aquinas may well be the most extensive ever undertaken. It is tied in closely with his notion of potentiality and his conception of the nature of things or entities. To the extent that he characterizes evil in relation to God's *intention* in creating a variety of things or creatures, his thinking echoes Biblical themes. Unfortunately, many of the other thinkers who view evil as privation have paid much less attention than Aquinas did to what the Bible says about evil and about God's work as Creator.

III

The view of evil as privation is almost invariably associated with the Platonist tradition — and rightly so. But what, exactly, is the Platonist tradition? This question is not so easily answered. Paul Oskar Kristeller observes:

> Plato's influence on Western thought has been so broad and profound, and in spite of occasional voices of dissent, so continuous, that a great contemporary thinker [Whitehead] has been able to state that the history of Western philosophy may be characterized as a series of footnotes to Plato. Yet if we examine the actual ideas of those thinkers who have professed their indebtedness to the Athenian philosopher or who have been called Platonists by themselves or by others, we do not only find, as might be expected, a series of different interpretations and reinterpretations of Plato's teachings and writings. We are also confronted with the puzzling fact that different Platonists have selected, emphasized, and developed different doctrines or passages from Plato's works. Hardly a single notion which we associate with Plato has been held by all Platonists.[5]

The diversity within the Platonist camp may help explain how it is that Schleiermacher, who was deeply interested in Plato and is often described as a Platonist, comes up with a conception of evil other than the one here being ascribed to the Platonist tradition. The important thing to note is that Schleiermacher did not read Plato in the light of Neoplatonism but made an intensive study of Plato on his own. Hence C. W. Christian concludes: "Schleiermacher is, despite his misgivings about all attempts to characterize the divine, a Platonist and not a Neoplatonist."[6]

The view of evil as privation does not find much *direct* support in Plato's own writings, although some of his key statements do inform the overall outlook on evil that emerged in the Neoplatonist camp. I think of the much-quoted passage in the *Protagoras*: ". . . no man voluntarily pursues evil, or that which he thinks to be evil. To prefer evil to good is not in human nature; and when a man is compelled to choose one of two evils, no one will choose the greater when he may have the less."[7]

The key to the Neoplatonist view of evil as privation is the thinking of the third-century philosopher Plotinus, in whom we find a fusion of Platonist themes with elements of Aristotle, especially in the treatment of evil. George J. Seidel writes: "What Plotinus has done is to take the identification which Plato made between matter and evil, and the identification Aristotle made between matter and non-being, and join them together."[8] Still, despite Aristotle's contribution to the thinking of Plotinus, the tradition in which he stands is named after Plato.

When we deal with the problem of evil, the influence and importance of the Platonist tradition can hardly be overestimated. Yet Plotinus and his followers suffer from neglect: they are not as well known as they should be, given their enormous influence. R. T. Wallis observes: ". . . a survey of Neoplatonism's influence threatens to become little less than a cultural history of Europe and the Near East down to the Renaissance, and on some points far beyond."[9]

IV

The question of the Neoplatonist stand on evil is complicated by the role of Augustine, a towering figure who has long overshadowed Plotinus. In many treatments of evil, the view of evil as privation is simply associated with Augustine. Plotinus is then relegated either to the footnotes or to a passing mention in the text.

Such an approach is taken especially by thinkers who argue that there are essentially two positions on evil. One position is the Manichaean view that evil is something real, powerful, active. The alternative to it is the view that evil is *not* something real, that it is privation, non-being. In the latter view, the initiative comes from the side of goodness, which is the *active* principle. Peter Brown contrasts the two views as follows:

> Plotinus had argued, constantly and passionately, throughout his *Enneads*, that the power of the Good always maintained the initiative: the One flowed out, touching everything, moulding and giving meaning to passive matter, without itself being in any way violated or diminished. The darkest strand of the Manichaean view of the world, the conviction that the power of the Good was essentially passive, that it could only suffer the violent impingement of an active and polluting force of evil, was eloquently denied by Plotinus.[10]

When we ponder the utter contrast between these two views, we see why Neoplatonism was such a liberating force in the life of Augustine, and why he was initially willing to embrace it as the answer to the problem of evil. The Neoplatonist view therefore came to expression in his own earlier writings. But later in life, under the growing influence of the Scriptures, he began to develop a somewhat different view of the nature of evil, which I propose to examine in the next chapter.

V

The Neoplatonist conception of evil, then, has been articulated most clearly by Plotinus, who has not received sufficient recognition from scholars. His view of evil is rooted not in an ethical system but in a metaphysical system, an interpretation of reality with God at its center. John Baillie writes that "the Neo-Platonists centred their whole system on the complete identification of God with the Idea of the Good."[11] God — or Goodness — then becomes the key to spelling out evil's ontological status (or lack thereof). Plotinus's view of evil has been summed up as follows by P. V. Pistorius:

> Evil is nothing else than the fact that God is present in a varying degree in different entities, and the measure in which He is not present in any entity, is the measure of evil in that entity. Everything that we can see or think is consequently partially evil, because our thoughts and actions have to do with the world of sense, and everything in the world of sense participates in God and in matter, and is therefore partially good and partially evil. The imaginary point where God is not, and where there is therefore an absolute lack of reality, is absolute evil.[12]

The fundamental idea here is that everything that is, is good to the extent that it actually exists — and evil to the extent that it does not exist. Evil has no existence in itself. Mary T. Clark writes: "All this makes for a great optimism in Plotinian philosophy and moral life, explicable perhaps by the implicit assumption of the divine quality of the universe, the best of all possible worlds."[13]

Plotinus's vision of good and evil has maintained its hold on our civilization over the centuries and still has its defenders today. However, it has also come in for its share of criticism and scorn. Voltaire remarked: "Lucullus [a Roman general known for his wealth and the luxury in which he lived], in good health, partak-

ing of a good dinner with his friends and his mistress in the hall
of Apollo, may deny the existence of evil; but let him put his
head out of the window and he will behold wretches; let him have
a fever, and he will be one himself."[14]

VI

A philosophy with many detractors usually has a good deal of
appeal. Our age is much concerned with the question of "liberation" or "emancipation." In a two-volume work on Plotinus we
read that for Plotinus, the conflict with evil is a "process of emancipation."[15] The author, William Ralph Inge, identifies himself
elsewhere as a "Christian Platonist."[16] By this he does not mean
that he is a follower of Augustine; his allegiance is rather to
Plotinus, who did not claim to be a Christian. Plotinus speaks "in
words as true as they are consoling." In introducing Plotinus, Inge
explains:

> I shall endeavor to put before you the teaching of this great man, in
> the hope that you will find it, as I have done, full of intellectual light
> and practical guidance. Nor am I without hope that, as we study him
> together, we shall find in him a message of calm and confidence for
> the troublous time through which we are passing.[17]

In another work, written many years earlier, Inge affirms: "My
conviction is unshaken that in the religious philosophy which he
[Plotinus] bequeathed to the Catholic Church — for the Christians, whom he never deigns to mention, and not the school of
Iamblichus, were his true spiritual heirs — we may find a truer
view of God, Man, and the World than in the systems which are
now most in favour."[18]

Some of the metaphysical details of Plotinus's philosophy certainly seem antiquated, but the notion of evil as non-being has
a contemporary ring — especially if we substitute knowledge for
being, as many contemporary thinkers are inclined to do. (Ontology or theory of being is much neglected nowadays in favor of
epistemology or theory of knowledge; thus philosophical problems
are often reformulated in terms of the latter.) If we think in epis-
temological terms we could say that evil is non-knowledge —
in other words, ignorance. For many of our contemporaries, it is
axiomatic that knowledge is good and that ignorance or the lack
of knowledge is bad. I will have more to say about this matter in
Chapter 14.

VII

We have seen that there are Christians who call themselves Platonists. Is Platonism (or Neoplatonism) then *the* Christian philosophy? This is a subject for philosophical debate, of course, but it is at least true that various Christian thinkers have taken issue with Platonism and its presuppositions. Why the opposition to Platonism?

One way to get at the central issue in this debate is by way of the "implicit pantheism" in Plotinus.[19] *Pantheism* is a term that has been applied to a wide variety of thinkers. The broad use of the term gives rise to certain questions. Some thinkers distinguish between pan-theism (everything is God) and pan-entheism (all things find their unity in God). W. R. Inge maintains that we should speak of "true pantheism" or "genuine pantheism" only in connection with a philosophical outlook in which it is maintained that "every phenomenon is equally Divine as it stands."[20]

Granted, caution is called for in the use of this term. Perhaps we should ask: How does pantheism differ from monotheism? In pantheism, writes Thomas Molnar, the "clear distinction that monotheism makes between god and man naturally disappears. . . . What characterizes then this doctrine is the absence of any ontological distinction between the Absolute and the universe."[21]

The question of the ontological distinction between God (or the Absolute) and the universe is also a very important issue for Herman Bavinck, who does not wish to see Christianity explicated in pantheist terms in which the separateness of the Creator God is undermined. Bavinck writes: "The true religion distinguishes itself from all other religions first of all in this respect, that it conceives of the relationship of God to the world and to man as the relationship of Creator to His creatures."[22]

In his concern about the pantheism question, Bavinck was echoing his distinguished contemporary Abraham Kuyper, for whom the struggle against pantheism was a struggle to preserve orthodoxy. For Kuyper, pantheism was the outlook that removes "the absolute boundary between the *Creator* and the *creature*."[23] This ontological boundary must ever be respected:

> Between God and man there is a boundary that no one can transgress. God is, and ever remains, *God*, and the creature is, and must ever remain, *creature*. Any attempt to wipe out this boundary or to blur it will always have this result, that man winds up wanting to be like

God, while God and the divine are seen as no more than an elevated
and glorified form of human existence.[24]

VIII

In Calvinist circles, then, the critique of Christian Platonism begins with the question of boundaries. But there are other questions
to be raised as well. If the divine is everywhere, what place is left
for contingency, choice, and responsibility? Mary T. Clark writes:
"Because in the system of Plotinus the contingent has no place,
the reality of free choice cannot be philosophically recognized. The
result is that Plotinus does not distinguish moral evil from metaphysical evil."[25] Natural (metaphysical) evil is given primacy, and
there is ultimately no room for moral evil.

The theologian Charles Hodge also criticizes pantheism and the
view of evil as privation. This outlook, he complains, denies the
existence of evil and therefore destroys the basis for moral obligation. Hodge comes to the same conclusion as Clark:

> This theory tends to obliterate the distinction between moral and
> physical evil. If sin be mere privation, or if it be the necessary con-
> sequence of the feebleness of the creature, it is the object of pity rather
> than of abhorrence. In the writings of the advocates of this theory the
> two senses of the words good and evil, the moral and the physical,
> are constantly interchanged and confounded; because evil according
> to their views is really little more than a misfortune, an unavoidable
> mistake as to what is really good.[26]

If Hodge is right, Christian Platonism must lead to Biblically unacceptable consequences in such areas as ethics, society, and politics. The problem that arises is this: if natural (or physical) evil
is given primacy over moral evil (or sin), how is it possible to
apply standards or norms to human conduct?

CHAPTER SEVEN

EVIL AS ALIENATION FROM GOD: AUGUSTINE AND CALVIN

I

THE mind of Augustine is a river fed by three streams: Manichaeism, Neoplatonism, and the Bible. There is development in his thinking: he moves from Manichaeism to Biblical categories by way of Neoplatonism. Naturally, the earlier terms and themes are never entirely shaken off. This is a factor that complicates the study of Augustine's relationship to Neoplatonism.

Another complicating factor is the sheer vitality of the Platonist tradition. Is Christianity conceivable *apart* from Platonism? William Ralph Inge writes: ". . . I doubt whether anyone can be an orthodox theologian without being a Platonist. Our creeds are the formulae of victorious Platonism."[1] J. H. Muirhead concurs with this assessment: "Platonism might indeed be called the intellectual side of Christianity."[2]

Can Augustine be placed *outside* this tradition? There are many scholars who simply reckon him among the Platonists, and it is not hard to see why. Paul Oskar Kristeller observes: "Augustine's repeated assertion that Platonism is closer to Christian doctrine than any other pagan philosophy went a long way to justify later attempts to combine or reconcile them with each other."[3]

Because there is movement in Augustine's thought, various commentators have chosen to deal with him in terms of the type of thinking he was working *toward*. Stanley R. Hopper, responding to the claim that Augustine remained a Neoplatonic Christian all his life, writes: "No doubt this claim is excessive, as it does not take into account sufficiently the psychological or existential focus on the will which accompanies this Neoplatonic development, and which he steadily matured throughout his later works toward the primacy of the Biblical categories."[4]

No one would want to argue that Augustine managed to shake off the Neoplatonist influence and categories completely. Still, Augustine himself recognized that his earlier enthusiasm for the Platonists had led him astray on various points. In his *Retractations*, written near the end of his life, he confessed to being "displeased" on account of ". . . the praise with which I extolled Plato or the Platonists or the Academic philosophers beyond what was proper for such irreligious men, especially those against whose great errors Christian teaching must be defended."[5]

The Christian Platonists themselves admit to a gulf between Augustine and their way of thinking. A. H. Armstrong, for example, has made some surprisingly harsh comments about "objectionable" elements in the thought of Augustine.[6] And in a book which Armstrong co-authored with R. A. Markus we read: ". . . in spite of Augustine's closeness to Platonism, there is also an infinite gulf between the two."[7]

II

Just what was at issue between Augustine and the Platonists on the question of evil? Augustine himself points in the direction of the basic problem in an observation he makes about the Manichaeans: "The Manichaeans do not understand that, if the Devil is evil by nature, there can be no question of sin at all."[8] In the Manichaean viewpoint, there is no possibility of overcoming sin (and evil), for evil always remains what it was.

Essentially the same problem exists in connection with the Platonist tradition, where moral evil is subordinated to natural (or metaphysical) evil (see p. 56 above). Given this outlook, there is a sense in which evil can be fled, but there is no moral and religious struggle against evil. Augustine apparently sensed that when evil is defined essentially in metaphysical (or ontological) terms, whether as something positive (Manichaeism) or as a lack (Platonism), the Biblical concept of sin becomes inapplicable.

Augustine's response was to accept evil as privation, as something negative, in the context of ontology, while making it something positive and real in his ethics and theology. In other words, he distinguished between the existential significance of evil (see p. 24 above) and its ontological status. He did so by developing a doctrine of moral evil or sin, a doctrine in which evil is taken very seriously and is made more basic to Christian thought than the metaphysical concept of evil as privation. For Augustine, then, the evil we experience is not the result of some deficiency in our basic make-up or nature but the consequence of our perverse and corrupt will.

III

The Calvinist tradition has stayed close to Augustine on the question of sin and grace. Calvinism has characteristically chosen to deal with evil as the problem of *sin*. In other words, it has subordinated natural evil to moral evil, which is the reverse of what the Platonist tradition does. As we will see later, it was moral evil that brought natural evil into man's life.

Although there is much talk about "will" in connection with sin, the problem goes much deeper than will or impulse. Just as man is called to love and worship God with his whole heart, the sinner hates God with his whole heart. In this hatred lies his sin — even before any sinful act is committed. Herman Bavinck declares that sin is in essence "enmity against God."[9] Bavinck recognizes that there is a time and place for talking about privation, a concept useful for combating the Manichaean error that evil is inherent in matter, but sin is much more than mere privation. Sin is both an aversion to God and a conversion to the creature.[10] The sinner turns away from God by turning to the creature instead and making it the object of his worship and the basis for his security.

Sin is not just an act or a feeling in one's heart but a *condition*. The consequence and punishment to which sin leads, writes Abraham Kuyper, is "alienation from God, distantiation from God, being cut off from God."[11] The sinner alienates himself by his act of rebellion, and then finds himself in a state of alienation, needing reconciliation.

IV

This conception of sin as enmity against God leading to alienation from God has its roots in Augustine's thought. Two aspects ought to be noted: the *personal element* in sin and the *consequences* sin brings with it.

Regarding the personal aspect, we must never underestimate Augustine's genuine horror at sin, especially lust, the sin that had dominated his life for so long. Once Augustine attained the spiritual maturity to recognize how disgusting sin really is, it dawned on him what an awful affront it must be in God's eyes. Would the judge of all the earth remain unperturbed at the sight of man groveling in sin? How could sin help but create distance between man and God? A. W. Matthews rightly mentions the element of love in connection with Augustine's view of sin: "The heart of sin is the alienation from God which comes through misdirection of man's love."[12] Here the familiar comparison with adultery and the alienation in which it results comes to mind.

Sin brings about certain consequences: it shapes our situation. It is in this context that we must view natural evil, understood now as God's judgment in response to our sin. We *do* evil — and we *suffer* evil. We alienate ourselves from God — and we find ourselves in a state of continuing alienation unless God approaches us in grace.

Our condition of sinfulness, alienation, and judgment must not be understood in individualistic terms, any more than we should seek to understand God's continuing favor to this world individualistically. To make His plan of redemption possible, God allows His favor to rest on *all* men: He "makes his sun rise on the evil and on the good, and sends rain on the just and on the unjust" (Matthew 5:45). Theologians speak here of "common grace." We can also speak of "common judgment," for the effects of the curse that rests on creation are not wholly lifted for those who turn to Christ. God allows earthquakes to swallow "the evil and the good, the just and the unjust." In other words, God's people never completely escape the effect of natural evil in this life.

In Calvin's writings we find the sinner's condition described in terms of estrangement. When Christ descended into hell He was "estranged from God."[13] For Calvin, sin and the evil it brings upon the sinner cannot be understood in terms of privation. Elsewhere Calvin suggests that our iniquities "completely estranged us from the Kingdom of Heaven."[14] Here he echoes Isaiah 59:2, where we read: "Your iniquities have made a separation between you and your God."

V

There is another reason why the Calvinist and Platonist traditions are theologically unsuited to each other. The Calvinist tradition follows Augustine in making much of history and development. God establishes a relationship with man — not just with individuals but with humanity as such. He covenants with man even before the fall into sin and approaches him again after the fall to establish an abiding fellowship, this time on the basis of a redemptive plan involving the atoning work of Jesus Christ.

The God who covenants with man is a *person*. On this point Platonism, with its roots in Greek thought, had certain difficulties. Thomas Molnar writes that Greek philosophy made "titanic efforts to arrive at a clear formulation of a personal god, yet it remained forever attracted to the notion of the absolute existence of the cosmos."[15]

Neoplatonism, with its leaning toward pantheism, seems to have stood in the way of developing the notion of a covenant relationship between God and man. Hendrikus Berkhof observes:

> If creator and creation are to be thought of as together involved in one process, then the possibility of facing each other in a personal relationship is excluded. For a personal relationship is based on discontinuity. A God who forms a continuous and co-existing unity with his world cannot as a person and with his will stand opposite the world and the other. And man is then not God's partner but only his product.[16]

Augustine understood the need for a God who exists as a distinct person. Paul Henry points to the importance of Augustine's unique contribution: "As I consider the tremendous changes from pre-Christian to Christian Western philosophy, even in secular philosophy, I am more and more convinced that three concepts, unknown to the Greeks and, perhaps, to all non-religious thought, are inseparably connected: creation, history, personality." Henry argues that "there is an intimate connection, entirely unknown to the Greeks, between the terms creativity, historicity and personality. In Augustine these are all linked in his synthesis of the relations of God and man."[17]

Greek categories did not allow for personal or existential relations between the divine and the human. Augustine, by developing the notion of personality in connection with God, prepared the way for a theological articulation of the covenant relationship between God and man. Hence Augustine speaks of Adam's sin as covenant breaking,[18] even though the word *covenant* (Hebrew *berith*) does not occur in Scripture for the first time until Genesis 6:18, in connection with Noah. The issue here is not terminology but the nature of the relationship between God and man.

VI

That original covenant relationship between man and God needs emphasis, for it sheds light on the nature of sin (and therefore of evil) in the thinking of Calvin and Augustine. The covenant between man and God is a *personal* relationship. We may speak here of fellowship — and even intimacy. What the rupture of that fellowship led to was not just privation or a lack, leaving man as less than what he should be, but active hostility, enmity, alienation. Man became God's enemy. Neither before the fall nor after is man indifferent to God.

Here we see how important it is to avoid not just pantheism, which erases the boundary between man and God, making man a part of the fuller reality known as God, but also deism, which pictures God as supremely unconcerned about the works of His hands. What we call religion did not spring into existence after the fall as a means of redemption: religion is simply life before the face of the Lord. Religion is covenant, a response to God which is intended to result in blessing, as God showers His gifts upon man. Herman Bavinck observes simply: "In Scripture, the relationship to God which believers attain through Christ is usually referred to by means of the word *covenant.*" For Bavinck, true religion always involves covenant.[19]

All too often we are inclined to think of man before the fall as perfect, needing nothing. But this is not how Calvin viewed Adam: "Even if man had remained free from all stain, his condition would have been too lowly for him to reach God without a Mediator." Thus Adam was not self-sufficient; he needed God. Calvin tells us that when Adam was blessed, it was "not because of his own good actions, but by participation in God."[20]

The covenant blessing Adam received through his participation in God, his fellowship with God, could easily turn into covenant wrath. In other words, the possibility of the curse was also placed before him: "You may freely eat of every tree of the garden; but of the tree of the knowledge of good and evil you shall not eat, for in the day that you eat of it you shall die" (Genesis 2:16—17). Adam took the fateful step and alienated himself from his Maker, whom he then came to perceive as a threatening figure. He proceeded to hide from God, who sought him out and told him that all nature would suffer the effect of the curse he had brought down on himself and his descendants. Adam's alienation from his God would also lead to alienation from nature.

CHAPTER EIGHT

DIMENSIONS OF EVIL

I

IN this chapter I shall return to the types of evil discussed in Part I to see how they relate to one another. In the previous two chapters the relation between natural evil and moral evil has already come under discussion. We saw in the Platonist tradition a tendency to subordinate moral evil or sin to natural evil. Biblical talk about "sinfulness" is then interpreted to mean that man is imperfect, finite, subject to limitations which he experiences as oppressive.

The tradition of Augustine and Calvin follows the reverse pattern: natural evil is subordinated to moral evil or sin. Natural evil does not come into the picture until man's fall into sin. Then his creaturely limitations become burdensome. At the same time the world he inhabits is subjected to the curse that results from man's disobedience. Things are out of joint for human beings not just inwardly but also in their relations to nature, to other creatures, and to one another.

For the most part, our modern world seems unable to accept this subordination of natural evil to moral evil. Especially after World War II, the reality of evil is very difficult to deny. Still, modern man is reluctant to use moral and religious language to talk about evil. Hence he looks instead to other categories — such as the metaphor of illness.

The theoretical choice to be made with regard to evil is in some sense a choice between sin and sickness. Is man depraved or deprived? The Christian tradition has dealt with evil primarily in terms of sin or depravity, but modern man tends to rely on the illness metaphor and uses the language of sickness.

Susan Sontag, who has investigated this metaphor, writes:

Modern totalitarian movements, whether of the right or of the left, have been peculiarly — and revealingly — inclined to use disease imagery. The Nazis declared that someone of mixed "racial" origin was like a syphilitic. European Jewry was repeatedly analogized to syphilis, and to a cancer that must be excised. Disease metaphors were a staple of Bolshevik polemics, and Trotsky, the most gifted of all communist polemicists, used them with the greatest profusion — particularly after his banishment from the Soviet Union in 1929. Stalinism was called a cholera, a syphilis, and a cancer.[1]

Such language is not restricted to political propagandists, however. Various social evils are often described in the language of illness. And when the categories of moral evil and natural evil are run together, the guilt normally associated with moral evil begins to cling even to genuine illness. In short, the category of illness grows, as psychological language comes to span both sin and sickness. Sontag observes:

> Illness expands by means of two hypotheses. The first is that every form of social deviation can be considered an illness. Thus, if criminal behavior can be considered an illness, then criminals are not to be condemned or punished but to be understood (as a doctor understands), treated, cured. The second is that every illness can be considered psychologically. Illness is interpreted as, basically, a psychological event, and people are encouraged to believe that they get sick because they (unconsciously) want to, and that they can cure themselves by the mobilization of will; that they can choose not to die of the disease.[2]

II

The question of the relation between illness and evil cannot be avoided in a Christian treatment of evil. Christians may wish to regard illness as a phenomenon that enters creation after the fall into sin, but they must ask themselves whether such a view can be reconciled with Scripture. The Bible does not give us much medical and biological detail about the world Adam originally inhabited, but it does tell us that Adam was placed among the plants and animals. We are told that God looked over everything He had made and declared it "very good" (Genesis 1:31).

The question that arises here is whether there was death among the plants and animals before man's disobedience brought the curse over creation. To this question one might respond by asking whether an organic realm is conceivable without death. Herman

Bavinck did not think so: "Pain and death seem to be necessary by nature for the physical organism."[3] Moreover, if there was no death among the plants and animals, Adam would have had a hard time understanding God when He told him not to eat the fruit of the tree of the knowledge of good and evil: "In the day that you eat of it you shall die" (Genesis 2:17). Adam must have observed that death came to the animals — perhaps in the relatively painless manner suggested by W. H. Hudson (see p. 14 above).

It is also important to note that man was not created and placed in the garden of Eden to live in a state of unchanging perfection. He was given a task (the cultural mandate) in the expectation that he would undergo a development, a history. Bavinck therefore speaks of man's original condition as provisional and temporary: man stood at the *beginning* of the route he was to travel. "At the time the world was only at the beginning of its development and was therefore perfect not in degree and measure but in its nature and character."[4] As for Adam, his condition was one "which could not remain as it was, but would have to either lead to a higher glory or to a fall into sin and death."[5] Klaas Schilder speaks of "growth" in connection with Adam in Paradise: "He was good, sound, but he still had to grow, to become a full man of God."[6]

This understanding of the nature and life circumstances of the first human beings must be read as a rejection of the criticism raised earlier by John Hick (see p. 47 above). Hick makes the category of natural evil too broad and includes within it man's creaturely limitations, which should not be viewed as inherently evil.

III

Fundamental to the Calvinist tradition and its understanding of evil is the doctrine of the covenant, in terms of which the relationship between man and God is to be understood. Religion (i.e., the relationship between man and God) did not become necessary *after* the fall as a means of redemption; rather, religion is to be understood as the (covenantal) fellowship and intimacy between man and God that already began in the garden of Eden. God did not create man to watch him from a distance but to receive his worship and adoration. The purpose of creation is that God be glorified.

The covenant relationship between man and God has a certain structure. Faithfulness to the covenant leads to blessing for man. By virtue of such a promise of blessing, theologians have sometimes spoken of a "covenant of works" in which Adam lived before the fall. But the covenant, as a relationship presupposing freedom, also included provision for the possibility of disobedience. Unfaithfulness on man's part would lead to judgment, punishment, death — in short, the curse.

In Genesis 3:16—19 we read about changes in man's situation as a result of his fall into sin. The words we find there should not be regarded as recording a decision made by God *after* man fell into sin; rather, they should be read as a declaration that the terms of the covenant between man and God would now go into effect by way of curse. In other words, these words are to be understood more as a reminder to man of the consequences of disobedience than as an exhaustive list of things that were being instituted for the first time.

This is to say, essentially, that God foresaw the fall and the possibility of sin and provided for it in the structure of the creation order. In other words, although God did not will sin, He did will and create the possibility of sin when He chose to create free creatures capable of living in covenantal fellowship with Him. Herman Bavinck explains: ". . . yet He did not will evil in the very same manner in which He willed good; He takes pleasure in the good, but He hates the evil with a divine hatred."[7] We must not forget that the Lord declared by way of His prophet: "I have no pleasure in the death of the wicked" (Ezekiel 33:11).

Here we approach the mystery that can never be dispelled when we deal with sin and evil. We cannot help but ask: Why? Augustine offers the only answer that seems possible to me: "He judged it better to bring good out of evil than not to permit evil to exist at all."[8] When it comes to the fall of Satan, Augustine offers the same perspective:

> Although God foresaw that some of these free angels would try to lift themselves up to a level where they might find their happiness in themselves alone and so abandon God, their only good, God did not take away their freedom. He judged it better and more in accord with His power to bring some greater good even out of evil than to permit no evil whatsoever.[9]

IV

What is the connection between sin and evil? Is *sin* a theological term, while *evil* is more properly a philosophical concept? I don't believe so. To trace the connection, we must recognize that the evil we *commit* (i.e., sin) leads to the evil we *suffer* (i.e., judgment), including natural evil.

Herman Bavinck points to this relationship when he writes that sin is not always and solely a *deed*, something that we will (which is the Pelagian view that Augustine combated), but also a *condition*.[10] Abraham Kuyper once used a different comparison: sin is like fire.[11] We all know what happens when a fire gets going: it burns out of control, with disastrous consequences all around.

Misconceptions can easily arise here, however. We sometimes think of the consequence of man's fall into sin as some sort of cataclysmic upheaval in creation. The Bible does not speak of such an upheaval; it simply mentions that the curse resulting from man's disobedience went into effect. This was not a second creation to which certain types of creatures and entities may trace their origin. Bavinck observes: "All the essential constituents [of this world] that exist now also existed before the fall."[12]

Likewise, we must not conceive of the fall as *removing* certain constituents or elements from creation. Man was still man after the fall; no aspect of his nature had been stripped away. The change in man was a change in the *direction* of his life. Instead of directing his love and worship and service to God, he focused it on an idol. Writes Bavinck: "When man transgresses God's law, he does not cease being man; he retains his body, his soul, his capacities, his powers, his mind, his will, and so forth, but they all come to stand in the service of sin and work in a wrong direction."[13]

It is important to note that God's law, His creation order, governs not only the healthy unfolding of the creation within the pattern of covenant blessing but also the outworking of the curse upon creation. In other words, the development of sin with its consequences is also subject to God's law. Bavinck explains:

> Sin, too, arises and develops in accordance with fixed law — not the laws of nature or of logic but the laws which are built into ethical life and continue to operate in destruction. Sickness, decay and death are the diametrical opposites of health, development and life; yet the for-

mer are governed from beginning to end by fixed laws no less than the latter are. Thus there is also a law of sin that governs the history of sin in man and in humanity. What the lawful element in sin proves is that God rules in and over sin as King. A human being who sins does not make himself free and independent of God; on the contrary, although he was once a son, he becomes a slave.[14]

In other words, degeneration and decay are law-governed phenomena. This applies not only to individual creatures but to humanity's history and to the realm of plants and animals. Nature, after all, is paying the penalty for man's sin and disobedience.

Hence we may conclude that man's powers have declined since the fall into sin. He no longer adjusts as smoothly and harmoniously to the organic realm in which he participates as he once did. This degeneration, leading to an increase in suffering (natural evil), is part of the price we pay for sin. Yet it all comes about not through a cosmic upheaval but through the operation of the laws which we refer to as the creation order, laws present from the very beginning.

Much of what is called natural evil, then, is this lack of adjustment, this disharmony. The human body is now vulnerable to attack by all sorts of disease-producing micro-organisms that cause us misery and destroy us. Instead of exercising dominion over nature, we are susceptible to its destructive powers. The earth swallows man whole, and his flesh rots. All of this was *possible* before the fall, but it only became *actual* as part of the momentous train of events set into motion by man's rebellion against God. Nature itself acts as a chastening rod in God's hand.

V

Viewed in global perspective, then, moral evil and natural evil relate to each other as sin and judgment. What about the category of demonic evil?

There is a sense in which demonic evil falls under the same heading as moral evil. In fact, the question of the origin of sin and evil needs to be pushed back beyond the first sin of Adam and Eve. John Murray writes: "Sin was present in the universe prior to the fall of man. Already there was a kingdom of sin and of evil. Of that kingdom Satan was the head. . . ."[15]

The reason why Satan's rebellion and man's sin cannot ultimately be dealt with under one heading is that Satan and his fallen angels are not united with our human race. Our fall does not affect them, and our salvation does not include theirs. God has chosen to keep the problem of Satan's rebellion separate.

We also need to keep demonic evil separate from human evil because of its great power and potential for harming us. The demonic realm derives part of its power from its incalculability. We have little solid knowledge of Satan and cannot map out a strategy against him in the same way that we can develop a strategy to defend ourselves against the threat posed by sinful human beings. The best we can do is to pray daily: "Deliver us from the evil one." In Christ there is protection from Satan.

The reality and threat of Satan should never be minimized. Yet there is very little we are able to say about him theologically. God willed the possibility of sin in Satan's case as well, and we must believe that He uses even Satan's wickedness to achieve His grand design.

A final word of caution about demonic evil is in order: we must avoid any preoccupation with it, lest we fall under its sway. We know Satan is busy as a tempter, but we may not transfer responsibility for our sins and shortcomings to the demons. The devil may influence and even injure us, but he has *not* been given power over us. Those who have heard the Word need not be deceived by Satan's lies.

VI

At various points I have indicated that it is not adequate to speak of sin and evil essentially in terms of privation, despite the fact that such a view has won considerable acceptance in Christian circles, both Catholic and Protestant. Although there is indeed a sense in which the fall into sin represents a loss, we must also recognize evil as a great power in this world, a power that will eventually be judged and destroyed.

What the privation view of evil wishes to stress, presumably, is that sin is not something created by God. Since there is no other creator, the logical conclusion is that sin is uncreated. The intention behind this line of argument is laudable, yet it allows for a certain misconception.

Religion, our covenant relationship with God, is not a *part* of life but embraces *all* of life. Sin, as a reversal or a turning away from God, affects *all* of life as well. If life *is* religion, that is, service of God and fellowship with God on the believer's part, we may say that life *is* sin for those who live in rebellion against God.

Religion is not a mere part of life, only one among other parts that remain unaffected by the fall into sin. Our fall, our depraved (sinful) state, is *total*. Hence our renewal is total as well.

One of the dangers of the deprivation theory of sin and evil, then, is that it suggests that sin and the service of God are not total but *partial*. Sinfulness on man's part means that some aspect of life is missing or absent, while religion is taken to be an aspect of life beyond the "natural" aspects which believers and unbelievers have in common. In short, the Calvinistic doctrine of total (pervasive) depravity does not leave room for the concept of sin as deprivation.

VII

Sin and evil do not have an origin or cause in the strict sense. God created the possibility of sin but did not actually bring it into being. We can point to a beginning of sin in the rebellion and disobedience first of the angels and then of man, but this is not yet to indicate a cause.

Sin is linked to our freedom. We may generalize about the free acts of human beings, but we can never really explain them. Why did Adam sin instead of continuing in the path of obedience? We can give no explanation. We can perhaps "understand," and we may have to admit that we might well have done the same thing in his place, but his free act has no ground outside itself. Adam and Eve sinned — that's all we can really say.

VIII

Much modern thinking does not respect freedom but is convinced that any being that is both good and free will follow a path that is predictable in principle. Therefore various thinkers have sought to determine what God would have had to do if He were truly both good and free. We should note that a curious reversal of perspective takes place here: man's happiness becomes God's end.

The Calvinist tradition has always made much of God's freedom. It has spoken of that freedom as God's "sovereignty." That sovereignty is not just power; it is also God's good pleasure, which man may not question. Scripture places God's glory at the center, and this center has become the starting point in Calvinist reflection. God's glory is the ultimate purpose of all His deeds of creation and redemption.

The Calvinist starting point has some definite consequences for the question of sin and evil in human life. Charles Hodge writes:

> The glory of God being the greatest end of all things, we are not obliged to assume that this is the best possible world for the production of happiness, or even for securing the greatest degree of holiness among rational creatures. It is wisely adapted for the end for which it was designed, namely, the manifestation of the manifold perfections of God. That God, in revealing Himself, does promote the highest good of His creatures, consistent with the promotion of His own glory, may be admitted. But to reverse this order, to make the good of the creature the highest end, is to pervert and subvert the whole scheme; it is to put the means for the end, to subordinate God to the universe, the Infinite to the finite.[16]

Hodge's perspective is not widely accepted today; the ethical theory known as utilitarianism has long been pushing it aside. Utilitarianism asserts that human beings must always choose the course of action that will bring as much happiness to as many people as possible. This general rule becomes a norm or standard for defining goodness and righteousness.

John Calvin, proceeding from the sovereignty of God, refused to allow any human conception of goodness or justice to define God's nature or character. Thus Calvin was well aware of the issue raised in our time by John Hick, who argues that the Biblical account of God's dealings with man cannot be accepted as it stands because it presents God as pursuing a policy which would be branded unjust by most people today (see p. 47 above). Calvin rejects this line of argument out of hand and claims that it works just the other way around: it is *God* who defines goodness and righteousness:

> Foolish men contend with God in many ways, as though they held him liable to their accusations. . . . If thoughts of this sort ever occur to pious men, they will be sufficiently armed to break their force even by the one consideration that it is very wicked merely to investigate the causes of God's will. For his will is, and rightly ought to be, the

cause of all things that are. . . . For God's will is so much the highest
rule of righteousness that whatever he wills, by the very fact that he
wills it, must be considered righteous. When, therefore, one asks why
God has so done, we must reply: because he has willed it. But if you
proceed further to ask why he so willed, you are seeking something
greater and higher than God's will, which cannot be found.[17]

Calvin's approach to this central issue is flatly rejected by various thinkers who insist on imposing human ethical sentiments
on God. The result, of course, is not just a rejection of Calvin but
a rejection of the Scriptural picture of God. George C. Brooks, for
example, argues that the God of Easter, the God who sacrifices
His own Son, has "no finer instincts than a primitive man." He
continues: "Easter, it seems to me, asks us to worship a God
Whose moral sense is less than our own. I think it is moral blind-
ness when Christian worshipers are unable to see this." Brooks
concludes: "Easter theology is, in short, self-defeating. It deadens
our moral nature and leads us to accept *any* picture of God if only
it proves that Jesus' death and resurrection guarantees us life after
death and grace from sin."[18]

John Hick thinks along similar lines. In orthodox Christian
theology, Christ's death on the cross is viewed as a necessary step
in the redemption of sinners. Yet Hick speaks of it as "a case of
utterly unjust suffering" and as "an evil than which no greater
can be conceived."[19] To him it is inconceivable that Christ's agony
could be part of God's plan for punishing sin and working
redemption.

Like many others, Hick brings "moral" arguments against God's
dealings with mankind as those dealings are traditionally understood: ". . . the policy of punishing the whole succeeding human
race for the sin of the first pair is, by the best human moral
standards, unjust. . . ." Hick speaks of God as "the Lord of a
chosen in-group whom He loves, who are surrounded by an alien
out-group, whom He hates."[20]

In such thinkers we see how ethical considerations become uppermost: sentiment triumphs over justice. Man is placed in the
center, and all of theology (including the conception of God) is
made subordinate to *man's* happiness (utilitarianism). I have not
yet read a suggestion to the effect that if God is truly good and
free, He is obliged to create an infinite number of human beings
on whom to shower His grace, but such a demand would appear

to be in order once we begin using human moral standards to define God.

At bottom, of course, the complaint is not that God does not do as much good as He might; the real complaint is that He chooses to punish sinners. Christ's death on the cross makes sense only in the light of God's determination not to let sin go unpunished.

Why this opposition to the idea of punishment? The opposition seems strange if one begins with the notion of sin as a rebellion against God through which natural evil comes into the world. On the other hand, if natural evil is made primary and sin is viewed as man's inescapable finitude, punishment does indeed appear to be inappropriate. If man can never overcome his finitude and sinfulness (despite the "growth" he may achieve), it does not seem right that he should be punished for it. In short, if natural evil is made the most basic type of evil, one is likely to wind up with John Hick's "God of love," who saves all men.

IX

The theological position that all men must be — and will be — saved is known as universalism. Frank Hugh Foster regarded universalism to be essentially "an English distortion of Calvinism." The opponents of Calvinism in New England, according to Foster, "ethicized theology."[21] Herbert Wallace Schneider sums up the great transformation in New England as follows: ". . . Puritan benevolence or love had found its object in the excellence and glory of God; now benevolence itself was deified."[22] The idea of God was recast as the idea of goodness (see p. 53 above).

Abraham Kuyper, whose own background was liberal theology, was intimately acquainted with the "ethicizing" tendency, which he associated with pantheism and its destruction of the ontological distinction between Creator and creature (see pp. 55–56 above). He writes that it is an "iron law" of pantheism that "the boundary between religious and ethical life is eliminated and that all religious phenomena are turned into *ethical phenomena*."[23]

To reflect on the nature of evil is at the same time to reflect on the ultimate ground of goodness. If goodness is rooted in God, the possibility of evil must also be rooted in God. But if goodness is rooted in man, the very possibility of evil becomes elusive.

Then the suggestion that evil is nothing, non-being, illusion becomes attractive.

The tendency to put man at the center of all thinking is deeply rooted in the human heart. Arthur Custance refers to this tendency when he writes that human beings are Arminians (and Pelagians) at heart. He argues that in the final analysis, the alternative to the theology of grace found in Augustine and Calvin is a "Christianized humanism."[24]

Arminianism (i.e., the doctrine that Christ died for all men, although not all men are saved) and universalism (i.e., the doctrine that all men are saved) are both reactions against Calvinism; they are two steps on the road to be followed when God's sovereignty is rejected. The doctrine of the Trinity next becomes superfluous — Unitarianism. And once Unitarianism is embraced, it is but a short step to an unabashed Humanism with man self-consciously at the center. These steps are illustrated in the development of Calvinist theology in New England (see Chapter 15 below).

But such an outlook leaves man with no ultimately satisfying response in the face of the problem of evil. Evil cannot be denied, and man cannot overcome it unaided. Only the sovereign God revealed in the Bible is able to vanquish evil — and He will do so. In the meantime we must learn to live with evil.

PART THREE
BEHOLDING EVIL

GIVEN any but an utterly unrealistic definition of evil, we must conclude that evil is all around us. We simply cannot help noticing it. But *should* we behold evil and depictions of evil? Is it good for us to behold evil? May we ever take pleasure in doing so?

There are a number of contexts within which this issue might be raised. One of the first that comes to mind is the much-discussed question of the depiction of sex and violence (Chapter 9). Generally speaking, we are inclined to say that there are dangers in beholding evil in such forms.

When it comes to suffering and illness (Chapter 10), we must take an entirely different approach: beholding evil becomes an obligation in certain circumstances. Much as we would like to avert our eyes when we see the human body ravaged by disease and deformed by genetic disorders, we must reach out to suffering human beings in love and make their lives part of our own. We may not shun them.

As for beholding conflicts and spectacles (Chapter 11), neither a simple yes nor a simple no will do. There certainly are spectacles that demean those who watch, but some spectacles and manifestations of conflict should indeed be scrutinized. An interest in struggles of certain sorts should not be entirely discouraged or ruled out as wrong.

Finally, we must ask about the appropriateness of imagining and depicting forms of evil in art works and in historical narratives intended for a wide reading audience (Chapter 12). How about the depiction of sexual acts and relationships? Is there positive value in depicting suffering and struggle? Where does the suffering of Christ fit in? Is there any place for the glorification of heroism?

CHAPTER NINE

PORNOGRAPHY
AND
VIOLENCE

I

THE contemporary conception of pornography has undergone a development that reflects changes within our society and modern consciousness. George P. Elliott defines what had once been the traditional understanding of pornography: "Originally the word pornography meant a sort of low erotic art, the writing of and about whores with the intention of arousing a man's lust so that he would go to a whore."[1]

Today the term *pornography* has a more sinister ring to it. In the popular mind we often find sex and violence linked; people expect hard-core pornography to display masochistic sex and brutal sex. Such pornography is regarded less as an incitement to sexual activity than as something to be watched (or read) and enjoyed for its own sake; in other words, it is entertainment.

The widespread public anger at pornography is partially rooted in this linking of sex and brutality. People fear that the circulation of pornographic materials will undermine moral values and send our society drifting further and further in the direction of anarchy. The "dirty pictures" of the past seem quaint and almost harmless by comparison.

II

Although we live in a generally tolerant society, pornography is today being attacked from many quarters. Parents and public officials demand laws against it, while professors criticize it on literary grounds, dismissing it merely as poor literature.

A significant line of criticism has been developed by Steven

Marcus, who links pornography with utopia (literally *no place*) to form what he calls "pornotopia." Pornographic stories, he complains, have no real setting, and even if a setting is cited, the writer does not weave the setting into the story. The result is a dreary sameness. Moreover, time does not properly function as an organizing principle. Marcus complains: "A typical piece of pornographic fiction will usually have some crude excuse for a beginning, but, having once begun, it goes on and on and ends nowhere." We are treated to endless repetition in which time is not a factor. Marcus observes: "To the question, 'What time is it in pornotopia?' one is tempted to answer, 'It is always bedtime,' for that is in a literal sense true."[2] In short, pornography ushers us into an unreal world.

Susan Sontag has responded to Marcus's critique by suggesting that the pornographer's detachment from the usual parameters of space and time should not by itself keep us from treating pornography as serious literature. She makes this point by comparing pornography to a form of literature that receives much more favorable treatment at the hands of critics — science fiction:

> There is nothing conclusive in the well-known fact that most men and women fall short of the sexual prowess that people in pornography are represented as enjoying; that the size of organs, number and duration of orgasms, variety and feasibility of sexual powers, and amount of sexual energy all seem grossly exaggerated. Yes, and the spaceships and the teeming planets depicted in science-fiction novels don't exist either. The fact that the site of narrative is an ideal *topos* [place] disqualifies neither pornography nor science fiction from being literature.[3]

The fact that so much pornography turns out to be poorly written and lacking in genuine aesthetic imagination does not by itself bar pornography from the category of literature. It is difficult, to say the least, to make pornography and literature into two categories to be kept fully separate. We must not rule out the possibility that literary works of unmistakable merit might contain clearly pornographic elements, chapters, or scenes.

III

Sontag has more insightful comments to offer on the nature of pornographic writing. She makes a further helpful comparison:

In some respects, the use of sexual obsessions as a subject for literature resembles the use of a literary subject whose validity far fewer people would contest: religious obsessions. So compared, the familiar fact of pornography's definite, aggressive impact upon its readers looks somewhat different. Its celebrated intention of sexually stimulating readers is really a species of proselytizing. Pornography that is serious literature aims to "excite" in the same way that books which render an extreme form of religious experience aim to "convert."[4]

What Sontag is suggesting is that some writers of pornography must be viewed as "evangelists" for their cause, which we might call "sexualism." (The word *sexism* signifies a different phenomenon.) *Proselytizing* (or evangelizing) is a significant term in this context, for there is more than sheer sexual delight in some manifestations of the sexual; various people believe there is sometimes a link between sexual ecstasy and religious ecstasy. Indeed, the former takes the place of the latter on occasion. William Sargant, who speaks of "sexual mysticism," observes:

If man is thought to rise to the level of the divine in mystical experience, it has been believed by millions of people that he can attain the same level in the ecstasy of sex. The experience of being swept away in an overwhelming tide of desire, which carries the lovers irresistibly along with it, which smashes down all barriers of convention, which the lovers themselves may realize will hurt others close to them, but which they feel powerless to control, long ago suggested to humanity that to be passionately in love is to be seized by a force from outside oneself, a force which is superhuman and in some religions divine. A lover traditionally behaves like a madman, another sufferer frequently regarded as possessed by a god or a demon, and lovers in orgasm behave as if they were possessed, trembling, writhing, groaning, crying out, as blind and deaf to everything around them as if they were no longer on any earthly plane.[5]

In the history of religion we find confirmations of the link to which Sargant points: there are false faiths which include sexual rituals (e.g., temple prostitution) in their worship. We see around us today considerable proselytizing or evangelizing on behalf of the false faith of sexualism, by which I mean the outlook that makes sexuality the basis of life's meaning and the channel for knitting human beings together. Given such an outlook, sexual ecstasy becomes the divine; it is the highest privilege given to man in this life.

IV

The point I am making is that much of the concern about pornographic literature in our society is misplaced — or perhaps I should say misdirected. The issue is not solely whether standards of taste and decency have been violated, or whether certain movies, books, and magazines are so explicit in their depiction of sex that they are apt to lead young people down paths of sin. No, I believe that the flood of pornography now washing over our society must be viewed above all as a flood of propaganda. Sexualism seeks converts.

Pornography aims to break down "taboos" by presenting us with the full range of sexual practices. George P. Elliott explains:

> Sexual taboos, like fashions in dress, are determined by local custom and have as little to do with morality as the kinds of clothes we wear. However — the argument goes — people frequently mistake these sexual taboos for ethical rules, and pass and enforce laws punishing those who violate the taboos. The result is a reduction of pleasure in sex and an increase in guilt, with an attendant host of psychological and social ills. The obvious solution is to abolish the taboos and so liberate the human spirit from its chief source of oppression and guilt.[6]

Elliott mentions Paul Goodman as an exponent of the "liberated" view of sex. Another is the Swedish physician Lars Ullerstam, who wrote a book some years ago pleading for a fully liberated and sexually open society — open to any sexual practice and quirk short of outright sexual violence causing damage to the body.

Ullerstam's book is not a piece of pornography by our usual standards. It bristles with technical terms as it works its way through the various deviations. Ullerstam's theme is the "erotic minorities." The "sexually orthodox," he maintains, are priviledged in our society; their sexual desires and needs are met, whereas the needs and desires of a great many other people are ruled out of bounds as "perversions." The so-called perversions should be encouraged, he argues, for they bring people happiness. (Here, of course, is utilitarianism again.) Children and young people should be included in this sexual liberation and should be free to receive sexual advances from older people. Not even homosexual seduction is ruled out:

Should loving genital manipulations occur between a child and an old man, we feel we have to call for the police, although anyone who takes an interest in child psychiatry should know that such behavior, generally speaking, does not harm the child in the least, rather the opposite being the case. Children have a craving for physical contact, and if they do not get it at home, they resort to outsiders.

Even if a homosexual seduction should have the effect postulated by the legislators [i.e., conversion to homosexuality], would this necessarily mean that it is to the disadvantage of the individual in question? Quite the contrary, could not this conversion prove to be a most fortunate event in his life? He is, after all, broadening the range of his ability to pleasure, and a whole new sex is suddenly put at his disposal. Perhaps the seduction saves the youth from lifelong misery as an impotent husband.[7]

Ullerstam, too, finds "spiritual" value in sexual experience. He notes: "There is a strong infusion of masochistic sexuality in the Christian mysticism of suffering, and it should be possible to read the story of Christ's Passion as masochistic pornography."[8]

Other "scientific" works dealing with sexuality aim at the promotion of similar goals. Even Alfred Kinsey, in his famous study of male sexuality (published in 1948), promoted a sexual ideology. The underlying purpose is especially evident in his treatment of homosexuality: Kinsey sought to undermine the notion of homosexuality and heterosexuality as two separate sexual identities. He insisted instead on a continuum as the model for understanding the variety he found in sexual roles and practices.

Kinsey's studies would not be branded as pornography. Yet such studies, especially the more recent of them, come close to pornography. First of all, many of them proselytize in favor of sexualism. Second, they include detailed, graphic accounts of actual sexual relations (neatly labeled "case histories"), which help boost their sales.

V

Many people in our society are in favor of banning pornography, arguing that it depicts things no one should behold. Given the nature and extent of pornography today, this might seem an attractive proposition, but there are dangers. For one thing, I don't believe that the line between pornography and literature can be clearly drawn. Even more important, I don't believe that the line between pornography and propaganda for the sexualist outlook on life can be clearly drawn. The censorship of pornography can all too easily lead to the censorship of other ideas that happen to be out of favor.

The censorship intended in the case of pornography is, admittedly, undertaken in the service of a good cause. Still, its results can be oppressive and harmful to society in the long run. The depiction of social and cultural values on American television has already given us a sample of how censorship can operate. The censor tends to supplant the author, rewriting and reshaping scripts so that they will have the officially approved impact on the public. The Soviet Union, not surprisingly, has wrestled with this problem for decades.

It should be remembered that censorship can cut both ways. Hence it can also be used in *defense* of the sexualist outlook. We see this possibility illustrated in the recent pressures to eliminate anything from television programs that might reflect adversely on homosexuality as a "lifestyle option." Ullerstam was not far from the mark when he made the "erotic minorities" a political issue in his book.

In short, once we recognize that pornography is — among other things — propaganda on behalf of a false faith (i.e., sexualism, with its glorification of promiscuity and its promotion of sexual deviance), we see that there are serious problems involved in any effort to ban it. Still, there must be some limits — moral and aesthetic limits, if not legal limits — on the depiction of sex acts. I will have more to say about this matter in Chapter 12.

VI

Our theme is learning to live with evil. In the assault on our sensibilities (and those of our children) made by the forces of sexualism, we must learn not to depend for relief too heavily on the government. Each family must assume the responsibility to avoid pornography. Today this clearly involves keeping various publications out of the home and staying away from certain television programs and movies.

Whether evil can be legislated out of existence is an age-old question. Christians have good grounds for believing that it cannot. However, the depiction of certain forms of evil can be restricted somewhat — at least in its distribution and sale — and that's what we should aim for in connection with pornography. We do have a right to demand, for example, that unsolicited pornography not be placed in our mailbox. And since children are impressionable, we also have a right to demand that they not be exposed to pornography.

Similar considerations apply to the depiction of violence, which is offensive in much the same way that pornography is. There is a place for violent scenes and allusions to violence in works of art, but violence for its own sake is clearly objectionable. Hence efforts have been made to reduce the amount of violence in television programs and to have the violence that remains placed within a context that renders it comprehensible.

Here again an outright ban is not feasible. In Chapter 12 I will comment further on the depiction of violence and the place of violence in historical narratives and in art.

VII

Two important ill effects are possible when we behold evil in the form of actual or depicted violence. These effects are similar to those caused by the depiction of sexual acts, but the parallel is not complete.

First, violence has the effect of desensitizing us. In drama, violence often has the most profound effect when it is used sparingly. The murder around which everything revolves in Shakespeare's *Macbeth* takes place offstage. In modern television programs, unfortunately, killings are so frequent that death seems to have no aftermath or consequences or emotional impact. In this respect art (or entertainment) is not true to life.

Second, the violence in books, movies, and television programs often expresses and glorifies a certain outlook on life, a religious vision which Christians find objectionable. The vision is that of Lamech, the figure early in Biblical history who sang a boastful song of revenge: "I have slain a man for wounding me, a young man for striking me. If Cain is avenged sevenfold, truly Lamech seventy-sevenfold" (Genesis 4:23—24).

In this glorification of violence, brute force represents the solution to life's disagreements and tensions. We are told that the strong prevail over the weak — that's simply how it is. On the national level, this abhorrent outlook on life takes the form of militarism. Much (although not all) of the fascination with war stories can be interpreted as a manifestation of the militarist spirit.

Lovers of peace may be utterly appalled at the religious vision that comes to expression in modern militarism as clearly as it did in Lamech's boast. Yet it cannot simply be outlawed. Restrictions on the depiction of violence may be necessary for television, but the voice that speaks up for the militarist outlook should not be silenced by the government. The militarist spirit cannot be legislated out of existence: Europe learned this lesson from the course of German history after World War I.

The militarist outlook must be combated first of all on the religious level; in other words, it must be attacked with spiritual weapons. Militarism, like sexualism, is a form of sinful rebellion against God — a turning away from God in order to seek certainty and assurance in the creature (i.e., military might) and to worship it instead.

CHAPTER TEN

SUFFERING AND SYMPATHY

I

IN the last chapter I talked about certain manifestations of evil that draw the attention of many people — depictions of violence and sexual acts. Obvious moral and spiritual dangers attend such depictions. Hence, it can be argued that we ought to avoid beholding such manifestations of evil.

In this chapter we will look at a different class of manifestations of evil — cases of pain and suffering. Although there are people who take pleasure in beholding the misery and agony of others, most people prefer to avert their eyes. Our tendency is to steer clear of fellow human beings who are suffering or in pain. When someone like Coleridge's ancient mariner tugs at our sleeve with a tale of woe to tell, our impulse is to hurry on.

The main point I wish to make in this chapter is that we must be willing to make the suffering of others *our* business. In other words, we may not simply avert our eyes and close our ears. If we are to live with evil, we must avoid some of its manifestations while resolutely confronting others. The suffering and pain of our fellow human beings falls into the latter category.

II

At the very outset of this book I drew a contrast between the strategy of denial, in which evil is not recognized for what it is, and the "anesthetic" approach to evil. Those who adopt the latter approach seek to numb or desensitize themselves. They do not deny the reality of pain; they simply take steps to keep from feeling the pain or misery inside themselves.

Certain professions are compelled to make considerable use of the anesthetic approach. John Keegan, in a book on warfare, discusses the aim of officer training and points to an interesting parallel:

> That aim, which Western armies have achieved with remarkably consistent success during the two hundred years in which formal military education has been carried on, is to reduce the conduct of war to a set of rules and a system of procedures — and thereby to make orderly and rational what is essentially chaotic and instinctive. It is an aim analogous to that — though I would not wish to push the analogy too far — pursued by medical schools in their fostering among students of a detached attitude to pain and distress in their patients, particularly victims of accidents.[1]

Soldiers and doctors would not be able to function successfully in their roles if they were highly sensitive to the pain and suffering of others. Still, the hardening they undergo in their training and their work can be a drawback in many of life's situations. Human beings need to be sensitive so that they can deal considerately with one another and understand each other. Of course, too much sensitivity can also be a hindrance.

III

There are reasons why we are so uneasy about beholding the pain and suffering of others. We are reminded of our own vulnerability to disease, injury, and ills of all sorts when we see our fellow human beings stricken. Because of the uneasiness which disease causes us, we tend to exclude and isolate the sick, thereby increasing the burden they have to bear.

A striking example of how we make the agony of illness even worse is leprosy. Perry Burgess describes leprosy as a "living death" and observes:

> From the beginning of recorded history its victims have suffered a fate more hideous than that of any criminal. Attacked by a disease that was rarely fatal but which often maimed and disfigured, its victims were objects of horror to themselves as well as to others. They were driven out of the land of the living, away from the company of their fellow men; forced to walk alone all the days of their lives; to bear in solitude their spiritual agony; to watch, uncomforted, their own physical disintegration.

And the sentence was without hope, without end. No punishment so ruthless, so devastatingly final has ever been devised by the most vicious tyrant as the human race has inflicted upon these unhappy people.[2]

Old age is not itself a disease, but it brings infirmities and limitations with it. For many people it means extra burdens that cause unhappiness. Powers that could once be taken for granted ebb away. A feeling of not being needed or useful sets in. The mental and physical decline that usually accompanies old age is also a manifestation of evil. Those who suffer the indignities of old age need our support and compassion. Yet we use all sorts of devices to deny old age, probably because the very existence of the aged reminds younger people that we are *all* subject to the ravages of time. Hence there is a strong tendency to set old people aside, to remove them to institutions or to rooms from which they may emerge only at set times. All too often the aged are treated like lepers: they are not welcomed among younger people who have difficulty accepting human frailty and mortality.

Simone de Beauvoir therefore speaks of a "conspiracy of silence" regarding old age. Many people prefer not to admit that there is such a thing as old age. Old age has become a taboo, an unmentionable. Beauvoir writes:

> What a furious outcry I raised when I offended against this taboo at the end of *La Force des choses* [a volume of her memoirs]! Acknowledging that I was on the threshhold of old age was tantamount to saying that old age was lying there in wait for every woman, and that it had already laid hold upon many of them. Great numbers of people, particularly old people, told me, kindly or angrily but always at great length and again and again, that old age simply did not exist! There were some who were less young than others, and that was all it amounted to. Society looks upon old age as a kind of shameful secret that it is unseemly to mention.[3]

IV

Those with apprehensions about reaching out to fellow human beings who are suffering sometimes wonder just what the sufferers want, or rather, just what it is that can help the sufferers. Naturally, those who suffer seek an alleviation of their pain and misery. Sometimes others can help them in this regard — with medicine, for example — and sometimes they cannot. But what can be done for those who cannot be helped medically? And what about people who wish to help but are not in a position to offer medical aid? What can such people do to reach out to fellow human beings who are in misery and anguish?

The story of Treblinka, the Nazi death camp in Poland in which the prisoners eventually revolted, may help answer our question. The Jews in the camp paid a horrible price for their survival: they had to help with the extermination of their fellow Jews. This caused them untold anguish. As they resisted and plotted and planned, what they sought was not an alleviation of their suffering or even an opportunity for a noble death. No, they were determined that word of their suffering should reach the world outside. One of the leaders of the rebellion explained it in this way to the others:

> We must not lose sight of the fact that our purpose is not to choose our own death, but to get some men out of Treblinka, and in sufficiently large numbers that at least one will survive and be able to tell the story. We are not desperate men! Our aim is not suicide! We have a mission to carry out. I'm not afraid to die. But I want one man to be able to tell the tragedy of our death.[4]

The rebels were determined to make their ordeal known; somehow they found comfort in the thought of the news getting out.

We also come upon this link between knowledge and suffering in a moving passage in the Bible. When God appears to Moses in the burning bush, He informs him that He has not ignored the plight of His people Israel under Egyptian oppression: "I have seen the affliction of my people who are in Egypt, and have heard their cry because of their taskmasters; I know their sufferings, and I have come down to deliver them out of the hand of the Egyptians" (Exodus 3:7—8).

V

Does the sufferer really want others (including God) to *know* about his plight? Or does he seek compassion, sympathy? I believe he seeks both, but the gulf between the two is not as great as one might think.

We often conceive of sympathy as a mode of feeling, and it

does indeed involve feeling. But it is also bound up with knowledge. Hence various philosophers have pointed to a connection between sympathy and the kind of knowledge known as understanding. They then link the two by speaking of "sympathetic understanding." Such knowledge, rooted in sympathy for others, plays an important role in history, art, and our day-to-day contacts with our fellow human beings.[5]

The original meaning of *sympathy* is to "feel with" someone. In other words, when we sympathize with someone, we seek to know that person's situation from within; we try to put ourselves in his place to get a sense of what he is going through. As we read a book about the horrible things that took place at Treblinka, for example, we try to develop a sense (however inadequate) of what it was like.

Those who suffer feel better for knowing that others have some idea of what they are going through and are willing to share in their suffering by sympathetically living through it. The Dutch speak of "meeleven," that is "with-living," sharing the joys and sorrows of others.

VI

To be genuinely sympathetic can sometimes be difficult. According to a widely quoted saying, "You have no right to criticize me unless you've walked a mile in my shoes." But who could ever claim fully to have lived within another's circumstances?

There are sufferers who say they get no support from others because no one knows what they are going through. "No one could possibly know what it feels like," they hasten to tell us. Their argument comes down to this: "If you have never experienced what I'm now going through, it's impossible for you to offer me comfort or to sympathize with me."

There is a grain of truth in such talk. Yet if these statements were indeed true, the world would be in a sorry condition. People would then be islands of private experience cut off from each other.

When we face this issue, we must avoid the mistake of thinking in black-and-white terms. It is naturally our own experience that is the basis for understanding others and reliving their experiences. We imagine what it must be like for others by calling similar experiences to mind. This is perfectly legitimate. We may at times have to say to a sufferer: "It's true that I have never faced exactly what you are now facing, but I have had an experience somewhat like it. Therefore I have some idea of how you must feel."

The background experience we bring to understanding includes not only our direct personal experience but also what we have experienced in a "second-hand" manner through literature, art, and narrative history. We may not know from personal experience what it is like to live the life of a slave, but if we read about the history of slavery we will at least have some idea. A man has no opportunity in his own life to find out what it is like to be a wife and mother, but a sensitive and true novel with a woman as protagonist might give him some idea. Our education, broadly conceived, helps us lay a foundation for sympathizing with others and understanding them.

VII

Similar considerations tend to color our relations with the dying and the bereaved. Once again our own vulnerability and mortality hold us back. There is as great a "conspiracy of silence" in connection with death as there is in connection with aging; we try to hide from the dying the knowledge that death is near, or, if we once admit death's approach, we refuse to talk about it. William F. May writes:

> Silence has its origin in the awesomeness of death itself. Just as the Jew out of respect for the awesomeness of God would not pronounce the name *Jahweh*, so we find it impossible to bring the word death to our lips in the presence of its power. . . . In the presence of death our philosophies and our moralities desert us. They retreat and leave us wordless. Their rhetoric — which seems so suitable on other occasions — suddenly loses its power, and for a moment we may well wonder whether they themselves are caught up in a massive, verbose, uneasy flight from death while we are left with nothing to say except "to say it with flowers."[6]

Those who wish to offer comfort and sympathy to the dying and bereaved must break this silence. They must be willing to confront the awful reality of death *with* those who immediately face it. Their words and gestures will not dispel death, of course, but for the dying there is comfort in the realization that others know and care. A complete avoidance of the subject of death often has the effect of increasing the burden being borne by a person who knows he is dying.

"I know their suffering," God said to Moses. This is basically the message we must get across to the suffering — to the sick, the dying, and the bereaved. "Your suffering is mine," we must tell them. And we must also assure them that God is watching them and knows what they are going through.

If we are to offer such support and comfort, we must not shrink from visiting the sick and beholding what disease is doing to their bodies. In many cases the sick are not a welcome sight; often we are horrified by the changes we see when we visit them in the hospital. Still, we may not avert our eyes.

And when the sufferer is so near death that he hovers somewhere between consciousness and a comatose state, we must still be willing to offer our presence. Verbal communication may be impossible, but a squeeze of the hand can mean a great deal. Moreover, some who are unable to speak can still hear. We need to get the message across to them: "I know your suffering."

VIII

Although some illness results directly from a sinful way of life, most of it is not connected with particular sins people commit. We do not reproach people for falling prey to cancer or multiple sclerosis or hardening of the arteries.

Yet illness, as a form of natural evil, is in a sense a judgment that rests upon the human race on account of sin. The judgment strikes some much harder than others, even though all are guilty.

When we ponder these considerations, we must bear in mind that there is a solidarity in judgment corresponding to the solidarity in sin. We are all responsible together for the sins of mankind, for the human race is one body. When Nazi Germany murders millions of Jews, we may not sit back smugly and say: "I had nothing to do with it. I would *never* do such a thing."

Just as there are common blessings (common grace) which God showers on all mankind indiscriminately in order to make His plan of redemption possible, there is "common judgment" resting on the whole human race and on nature as well. This is a point we need to bear in mind in daily life. When multiple sclerosis strikes my neighbor and not me, I have no right to conclude that he is a greater sinner than I am. All the same, I cannot escape the conclusion that human sin and guilt have something to do with his disease and suffering.

IX

The solidarity theme is also important when we consider the suffering of Jesus Christ. Some Christians place great emphasis on the need for joy in the Christian life, and we Christians do have much to rejoice about. On the other hand, since sin and its effects are still such a presence in our lives, we also have reason to be somber on occasion, especially when we think of the awful suffering and death of Christ.

We prefer the Easter joy of the empty tomb to the anguish we must feel whenever we contemplate the suffering servant whose body was broken for us. So horribly did He suffer that He became "as one from whom men hide their faces" (Isaiah 53:3).

Sometimes we are so eager to doubt the agony of Christ on the cross that we call His humanity into question. Did He really suffer just as we would have suffered under similar circumstances? And wasn't there anyone to "know" His suffering? John L. McKenzie writes:

> The Gethsemane narrative shows clearly that Jesus was as well acquainted with the loneliness of pain as anyone of us. . . . That he should have sought the mere presence of others at this time ought to be revealing. It is not a pleasure to feel the violent hatred of others, and to know that there are people who are convinced that your death will make the world a better place to live in. It is likewise no pleasure to know that those who are closest to you seem completely unaware of the weight which you carry. When this happens to us, we call it our private hell.[7]

In the light of the awful agony endured by Christ, there is no room for a "Christian masochism" or a false glorification of pain and suffering. When we meditate on our Savior's *via dolorosa* during the Lenten season, we also learn something about the sufferings of our fellow human beings and their need for sympathy and support.

We must not declare that *all* suffering has a redemptive meaning; Christ's sacrifice was sufficient to meet the conditions for our redemption. But we may — and should — proclaim that God "knows" our suffering and does not hide His face from His people when they are afflicted and cry out to Him in prayer.

The suffering of Jesus can be an inspiration to us. At the same time, it reminds us of the centrality of the mystery of evil. What is mysterious is not just the existence of evil but the manner in which God combats evil and uses evil to effect our redemption. McKenzie comments as follows on the suffering of Christ:

> In his sufferings we discern the gospel theme that suffering is a part of the reign of sin and death; it is evil, not good, and the heart of the mystery of our redemption is that we are saved through something which is involved with sin and death. The gospel does not require us to praise suffering or to affirm that it has a goodness which it does not have. Suffering is a part of the human condition, that condition which in biblical language is called a curse.[8]

Jesus tells us that the Son of man *must* suffer (Mark 8:31; Luke 9:22). Once man made that horrible choice for sin and rebellion, evil could not be purged from God's creation without great suffering. When we behold the suffering of Christ and the anguish of our fellow human beings as they face disease and death, we cry out: "How long? Hasn't the agony gone on long enough?" Only God knows the answer.

CHAPTER ELEVEN

CONFLICT AND SPECTACLE

I

WE have seen that some forms of evil draw the attention of people even though they would be better advised to stay away from them (i.e., pornography and violence), while some other forms of evil are repulsive, with the result that people prefer to avert their eyes and avoid involvement (i.e., misery and suffering). Yet there is much that falls between these two categories. One could point to many spectacles and forms of conflict that have attracted widespread attention, even if there were indeed people who refused to become interested.

Showmen know that people love to see something new and out of the ordinary. One of the most successful acts in entertainment history was a nineteenth-century midget known as General Tom Thumb, who made appearances in North America and Europe under the sponsorship of P. T. Barnum. The midget was in no way misshapen or deformed: the only unusual thing about him was that he stood a mere twenty-five inches.

Barnum and his competitors in the entertainment business had more than midgets on display. Another of Barnum's successes was a pair of men who went through life anatomically joined — the original "Siamese twins," named Chang and Eng. Irving Wallace tells us how they were joined:

> From birth, they were united by a thick, fleshy ligament covered with skin, like a four-inch arm, connecting their lower chests. At first, this band held them face to face, but as they grew, it stretched to five and a half inches, allowing them to stand and move sideways. The joint was sensitive but strong. If it was touched at the middle, both boys felt the sensation. Yet so sturdy was it that if one of the Twins

happened to trip and lose his balance, the ligament held him dangling but firm.[1]

People paid good money to get a look at these unfortunates. And there are many more such examples that could be given, for it appears that there is no sight so hideous that people will not pay to see it. John Merrick, the grotesquely deformed "Elephant Man," also spent part of his life being displayed to others. More recently a stage play and a movie have chronicled his life.

In our time such human beings are rarely put on display. But other unusual people — greatly overweight, or with partial limbs, or discolored skin, or some other malady — are to be encountered in our streets. Well-mannered adults look the other way, while children stare and point. Clearly we do not know what to make of "freaks." Some people wish to abolish the term, but the people we apply it to remain what they are — different, and somehow not normal.[2]

II

Other spectacles in history, unlike human "spectacles" beyond human cure, have been entirely within man's power to eliminate. Their persistence was due solely to human perversity. The early mental hospitals fall into this category. Actually, they were not hospitals in any serious sense at all: they served only as warehouses for mentally and emotionally disturbed people who did not or could not function normally in society. Supposedly normal people would stroll through such institutions from time to time to gawk and laugh at the insane.

Such spectacles are no longer tolerated in our society, but others, involving animals, are. Lions and tigers are conditioned to perform on command to entertain us. Full-grown bears — magnificent, powerful animals — are decked out in dresses and straw hats and made to look comical as they clutch musical instruments. In many parts of the world, sad to say, fights to the death are still staged between combative animals or birds.

The most famous of the violent, bloody spectacles took place in the Roman amphitheaters. The gruesome battles and rending of flesh even pitted animals against human beings.[3] The cruelty and barbarism of the Romans who organized such entertainment is hard to understand, but similar impulses manifest themselves in human behavior today.

III

It would be easy to conclude that these spectacles, in which people have taken a malicious delight over the ages, are thoroughly reprehensible and have no legitimate place in human life. One is tempted to draw such a conclusion, and yet to do so is perhaps too simple. The human love of spectacles involves more than mere malicious glee. Our love of spectacles is also a factor, for example, in the complex phenomenon of warfare.

J. Glenn Gray, in his book on war, speaks of "the lust of the eye" in connection with battle and of the "secret attraction" of warfare. He tells us that many soldiers take delight in battle as a spectacle. The splendor of the spectacle may be understood — in part, at least — in aesthetic terms:

> Some scenes of battle, much like storms over the ocean or sunsets on the desert or the night sky seen through a telescope, are able to overawe the single individual and hold him in a spell. He is lost in their majesty. His ego temporarily deserts him, and he is absorbed into what he sees. An awareness of power that far surpasses his limited imagination transports him into a state of mind unknown in his everyday experiences. Fleeting as these rapt moments may be, they are, for the majority of men, an escape from themselves that is very different from the escapes induced by sexual love or alcohol. This raptness is a joining and not a losing, a deprivation of self in exchange for a union with objects that were hitherto foreign. Yes, the chief aesthetic appeal of war surely lies in this feeling of the sublime, to which we, children of nature, are directed whether we desire it or not. Astonishment and wonder and awe appear to be part of our deepest being, and war offers them an exercise field par excellence.[4]

Although Gray is a philosopher who brings in academic language here, he speaks against the background of his own experience in World War II. He describes how an attack on the French Riviera in which he himself was to participate made a deep impression on him:

> When I could forget the havoc and terror that was being created by those shells and bombs among the half-awake inhabitants of the villages, the scene was beyond all question magnificent. I found it easily possible, indeed a temptation hard to resist, to gaze upon the scene spellbound, completely absorbed, indifferent to what the immediate future might bring. Others appeared to manifest a similar intense concentration on the spectacle.[5]

Other soldiers who took part in World War II report similar

reactions. From the published diary of a German soldier we learn that the thrill of the chase and the sight of the tanks could be not just frightening but enchanting:

> You simply cannot imagine . . . what the concentrated fire of a reinforced motor battalion means; you think the world's at an end. The thunder and roar of the guns, the shots bursting as they land, the trails of tracers from the flak, the burning houses in the town, increased by the tracer shells of our artillery. It's frightful — and beautiful.

> After passing through the first village, we spread out over the fields. Beforehand we are assigned some tanks, and now we've spread out the tanks and other vehicles in a broad formation over the fields and are charging into the fleeing Russians. The order of the Companies and other units has got a bit mixed up in the intoxication of this fabulous chase, but it's wonderful to watch the vehicles tearing ahead. There ought to be some newsreel men here; there would be incomparable picture material! Tanks and armoured cars, the men sitting on them, encrusted with a thick coating of dirt, heady with the excitement of the attack — haystacks set on fire by our tank cannons, running Russians, hiding, surrendering! It's a marvellous sight![6]

The weapons of war are "engines of destruction," like the lobster in Theodore Dreiser's novel (see p. 13 above). The mobilization and movement of these engines of destruction can itself be an epic, unforgettable sight. Some memorable prose has been written to describe armies and armadas massing for battle. I think of the classic description of the invasion forces which the Allies assembled to throw against Hitler's Europe on D day, 1944:

> For now back in the Channel, plowing through the choppy gray waters, a phalanx of ships bore down on Hitler's Europe — the might and fury of the free world unleashed at last. They came, rank after relentless rank, ten lanes wide, twenty miles across, five thousand ships of every description. There were fast new attack transports, slow rust-scarred freighters, small ocean liners, Channel steamers, hospital ships, weather-beaten tankers, coasters and swarms of fussing tugs. There were endless columns of shallow-draft landing ships — great wallowing vessels, some of them almost 350 feet long. Many of these and the other heavier transports carried smaller landing craft for the actual beach assault — more than 1,500 of them. Ahead of the convoys were processions of mine sweepers, Coast Guard cutters, buoy-layers and motor launches. Barrage balloons flew above the ships. Squadrons of fighter planes weaved below the clouds. And surrounding this fantastic cavalcade of ships packed with men, guns, tanks, motor vehicles

upplies, and excluding small naval vessels, was a formidable array of 702 warships.[7]

IV

There are many who would defend this depiction of the Allied invasion force on both moral and literary grounds, arguing that it is not offensive or corrupting. Stories about armies and battles have always had a certain appeal. Although today we tend to turn away from warfare in horror and disgust, we would do well to reflect on the reason for its popularity. It seems to me that there are no simple answers available for the questions that arise here. Is it entirely to be regretted that historical books and movies dealing with savage, intense conflicts represent a favorite form of entertainment?

One of the most popular ways to entertain people is to present a story — whether history or fiction. And if a story is truly to be a story, it must have conflict, a clash of some sort between opposing forces, or perhaps opposing tendencies within a single person. Literary "conflict" is the struggle that grows out of the interplay of the two opposing forces in the plot of a story. It is conflict that lends interest and suspense to a story.[8]

An interest in the conflict that is essential to a story, then, should not automatically be ruled out of bounds. Neither should an interest in degeneration, whether in people or situations or entire societies. Degeneration often provides the setting for a story. One of the reasons for the appeal of the novels of Charles Dickens, for example, is the horrifying setting he chose for some of them. Dickens displayed the seamy side of Victorian England and won automatic sympathy for his characters by pitting them against a desperate environment. Kellow Chesney describes the slums of Dickens's London as follows:

> Hideous slums, some of them acres wide, some no more than crannies of obscure misery, make up a substantial part of the metropolis. Because they are so densely occupied they are profitable, and seldom cleared away except to make way for new thoroughfares and frontages. In big, once handsome houses, thirty or more people of all ages may inhabit a single room, squatting, sleeping, copulating on the straw-filled billets or mounds of verminous rags that are the only furniture. There are cellar-homes, dark, foetid and damp with sewage,

where women keep watch for the rats that gnaw their infants' faces and fingers.[9]

The interest many people take in such settings is not necessarily an expression of baser elements in their makeup. Sympathy plays a role here, since we like to see people succeed in the face of the forces arrayed against them. A rags-to-riches story always has appeal.

V

We cannot, then, rule out as wrong all interest in conflict and spectacles. Some of it is well-motivated. Still, much of it speaks poorly of us and should be discouraged.

Spelling out rules and guidelines is not easy. Even the rationale for urging people to avoid gawking at freaks and attending taste-less exhibitions is hard to formulate. It seems to me that some of the considerations we might apply are related to the arguments generally adduced against cruelty to animals.

There are laws that protect certain types of animals from certain types of mistreatment. For the most part, however, the law leaves us free to deal with nonhuman creatures (especially the smaller ones) as we please. Children still pull legs off spiders and burn grasshoppers.

I don't believe we should pass *laws* against every conceivable form of mischief, although such infliction of pain should clearly be discouraged by parents and teachers. Just how much pain is actually caused in such creatures is hard to say; it is often argued that the fish does not suffer from the hook in its mouth when the fisherman reels it in. But whether fish and insects and other small creatures suffer or not, the willingness to treat even spiders and grasshoppers in an inhumane manner testifies to an inadequate or underdeveloped sense of solidarity with all nature and responsi-bility for nature. In the final analysis, we must avoid inflicting needless pain or degradation on animals and insects out of respect for ourselves as sensitive and compassionate persons bearing the image of a merciful God.

The "common judgment" that affects the natural world and the animals in the form of natural evil is the result of our sin. James Orr reminds us that "nature is a sufferer with man on account of sin" and speaks of "a solidarity between man and the outward world, both in his Fall and his Redemption."[10] We must always bear this solidarity with nature in mind and do our best to ensure that, although the creatures of God inevitably suffer on our account, they are not subjected to any needless pain.

When we see deformed human beings (e.g., the former Thalidomide babies, now grown into adults), similar considerations apply. The natural evil that strikes them so severely could just as well have struck anyone else. All human beings are equally guilty by virtue of mankind's original sin. Yet certain unfortunates bear the mark of the curse afflicting the earth more than others.

There is no place for self-satisfaction on the part of those who are not deformed; rather, sympathy and a willingness to help share the burden are called for. This we see fittingly manifested in the recent measures undertaken to make public buildings accessible and usable for handicapped people in wheelchairs. Never may we make a spectacle of diseased or deformed people, for to do so is to increase their burden and to demean ourselves.

VI

The question of spectacles that do not involve deformities raises another set of considerations. Those who are drawn to spectacles involving great destruction may be worshiping raw power. The mushroom cloud of a nuclear bomb is an awesome sight, but we must not fall down in worship before the bomb's power to level and destroy everything in its path. War movies that enhance their popularity with spectacular bombing scenes can lead to the formation of a militaristic attitude, one in which it is believed that conflicts or disputes between people are best resolved through violence. The spirit of Lamech must not be allowed to take root in our hearts.

Some spectacles may display a power from an even more dangerous source — Satan. For centuries there have been people who were fascinated by the prospect of contact with the supernatural. Extravagant claims have been made by so-called mediums and witches. It may well be that most of those claims are utter nonsense; all the same, we should steer clear of any spectacle or form of entertainment that promises to reveal Satan and his power.

Satan is essentially foreign to our experience, and therefore his doings are incalculable. Since the Bible ascribes considerable power to him, we ought to give him a wide berth. The ultimate cosmic confrontation in the battle between good and evil involves Satan and Christ — not Satan and some zealous Christian who believes he can fight his way to sainthood.

VII

A type of spectacle that has not been touched on yet is competition. Competitive sports and activities are open to much abuse; the "winning is the only thing" philosophy is much with us. Naturally, we must stress that it is very important how one plays the game. Still, the object of the game is to win, and there is nothing inherently wrong with winning.

Any competitive activity involves conflict and tension, whether one competes against an opponent in chess or against one's own previous record in the high jump. This conflict and tension also makes such activities of interest to other people. There need be nothing unhealthy or wrong with competitive activities as forms of entertainment.

In some Christian circles there is a tendency to overreact against the excesses and abuses we find in professional and collegiate athletics. The distortions that are undoubtedly present should not lead us to turn sports like baseball and football into something that they are not. To play catch may be fun and good exercise as well, but there is much more than playing catch involved in baseball and football. The object is to score runs or touchdowns.

We should not forget that the language of exertion and training and strenuous competition is to be found in Scripture. Paul compares the believer to a dedicated athlete: "Do you not know that in a race all the runners compete, but only one receives the prize? So run that you may obtain it" (I Corinthians 9:24).

The Christian life is a race, a conflict, a struggle. To make it to the goal, we must do battle with the forces of evil. That battle, when properly waged, can even be a spectacle that inspires others to fight on to the finish.

CHAPTER TWELVE

IMAGINATION AND DEPICTION

I

ONE of the aims of education is to develop the power of imagination. We are sometimes told that television, which places an endless stream of concrete images before children, deprives them of the need to use their imagination and thereby does them a disservice. Children need to hear stories told or to read them in books so that they will have to imagine what the monsters and heroes look like.

Monsters and heroes may loom large in the make-believe world of the child, but they are also becoming of interest to *adults* in our time. The entertainment industry feeds us a steady diet of monsters and catastrophes. It is also rediscovering the appeal of heroes — after many decades in which the hero seemed irrelevant or obsolete in art.

The emphasis on the heroic and its significance was a major theme in the nineteenth century — especially in the writings of Thomas Carlyle. Carlyle spoke of "hero *worship*" and declared: "We all love great men: love, venerate and bow down submissively before great men; nay, can we honestly bow down to anything else?" For Carlyle the hero is not just *morally* elevating but has a *religious* significance for us: "Hero-worship, heartfelt prostrate admiration, submission, burning, boundless, for a noblest godlike form of man — is not that the germ of Christianity itself?"[1]

Although Carlyle's ideas are often ridiculed, the need for heroes is being rediscovered. We need political heroes so that leadership in government may again be viewed as noble and valuable service. We need to view police officers and other public servants as self-sacrificing heroes who aim to protect the public. We need to see heroism in the daily struggle of ordinary men and women. Even faithfulness and commitment within marriage and the family must again be depicted within the framework of the heroic.

Heroism can also be understood as courage in a time of suffering and adversity. Hostages are sometimes heroes. So are the sick when they inspire others by how they cope with their disease and suffering. Adults and children both need people to admire, examples to follow.

In some modern art and entertainment, then, the hero is being revived. This means that the battle against the forces of evil is being depicted in all sorts of forms and settings. Heroism as the good can emerge and show itself clearly only against the background of evil.

II

Heroism is also a theme in the Bible, where we find some of the greatest stories in all of world literature. Who could ever forget the encounter between David and Goliath? The Bible is full of fierce conflict and stirring spectacles. Think of the great battles, and the exploits of Samson. We see thousands upon thousands of people advancing through the wilderness on their way to a new land. The walls of Jericho collapse, and entire cities go up in flames. Those who are enchanted by spectacles will not find the Bible dull reading.

Yet the hero we meet in the Bible is not David or Samson or Elijah but God Himself. In church we sing the words of Psalm 78: "Let children hear the mighty deeds which God performed of old." What were those mighty deeds, and who actually performed them — God's servants, or God Himself?

The great act of God which is fundamental to the understanding of deliverance in the Old Testament is the exodus from Egypt. The climax comes not when the Israelites are finally given permission to depart but at the Red Sea, when the Egyptians pursue the Israelites to bring them back to a life of slavery. We all know the outcome: the Israelites pass through the sea safely, but the Egyptians drown when the walls of water collapse on them. Moses and the people then sing a song of praise to the Lord:

I will sing to the Lord, for he has triumphed gloriously;
the horse and his rider he has thrown into the sea.
The Lord is my strength and my song,
and he has become my salvation;
this is my God, and I will praise him,
my father's God, and I will exalt him.
The Lord is a man of war;
the Lord is his name.
Pharaoh's chariots and his host he cast into the sea;
and his picked officers are sunk in the Red Sea.
The floods cover them;
they went down into the depths like a stone.
Thy right hand, O Lord, glorious in power,
thy right hand, O Lord, shatters the enemy.
In the greatness of thy majesty thou overthrowest thy adversaries;
thou sendest forth thy fury, it consumes them like stubble.

(Exodus 15:1—7)

Such scenes in the Bible meet a deep spiritual need within us, the need to see the forces of evil overcome not as ignorance is dispelled but as an army is defeated in battle. There are personal forces behind much of the evil in this world. When the Bible tells us about the mighty acts of God and the struggles of His people in this world, it gives us a framework and perspective for interpreting and understanding the struggles in which *we* find ourselves involved today. In short, there is a reason behind all the depiction of evil in the Bible.

III

Many people — not just children — are inclined to think in terms of "good guys" versus "bad guys." The Bible also seems to interpret conflicts within such a framework. Yet we must be careful not to make the mistake of identifying the Israelites as "good guys" standing opposed to the Egyptians as "bad guys." In Scripture, the line between the forces of good and the forces of evil cannot be drawn quite so simply.

The real battle in Scripture is between God (the forces of good) and His opponents (the forces of evil). The leader of the forces of evil is Satan, whose name simply means *adversary*. Whoever stands in God's way is a satan, an adversary. At one point Jesus even found it necessary to say to *Peter*, "Get behind me, Satan!" (Matthew 16:23; Mark 8:33).

God joins His cause to the cause of the people of Israel — provided they are faithful to the covenant. The promise comes to them in *conditional* form: "But if you hearken attentively to his voice [the voice of the angel sent before the people] and do all that I say, then I will be an enemy to your enemies and an adversary to your adversaries" (Exodus 23:22). Much later, because of the disobedience and apostasy of His people, God declares through His prophet: "But they rebelled and grieved his holy Spirit; therefore he turned to be their enemy, and himself fought against them" (Isaiah 63:10). We may not simply equate the covenant people with the "good guys" or the forces of good.

The cosmic conflict between good and evil is a major theme in the Bible. Scripture does not give us an exhaustive account of this war, but it does relate certain episodes. It also tells us what the ultimate issue is when someone like Pharaoh becomes a "satan," an adversary standing in God's path: "And I will harden the hearts of the Egyptians so that they shall go in after them, and I will get glory over Pharaoh and all his host, his chariots, and his horsemen. And the Egyptians shall know that I am the Lord, when I have gotten glory over Pharaoh, his chariots, and his horsemen" (Exodus 14:17–18).

IV

As we consider the depiction of evil, we should bear this Biblical background in mind. When people today enjoy movies and books in which the forces of good engage the forces of evil in battle and defeat them, we should not view this as evidence of decay and degeneration. There is nothing wrong with taking an interest in what appear to be (fictional or real) episodes in the cosmic battle of good against evil.

It is interesting that the literature of World War II generates considerably more interest than that of World War I. I believe there is a reason for this. In World War II we seem to see clearly delineated forces of evil opposed by forces that, conversely, are clearly good. But in World War I both sides seem to share in the blame for the death and destruction.

We are sometimes wrong, of course, in identifying certain sides in a conflict as the forces of good or the forces of evil. My point is that we do have a tendency to view conflicts in such terms, and that this tendency is rooted in an awareness that there are battles between the forces of good and evil going on, battles in which we want to be on the side of good.

We relive those battles through our forms of entertainment. It is sometimes said that we "need" the Nazis as villains, and that if they hadn't existed we would have been forced to invent them. There is some truth to this, and therefore the contemporary preoccupation with Nazism as a manifestation of the forces of evil is not to be deplored — provided we do not equate being a Nazi with being a German.

Children are especially given to involving themselves in the dynamics of the struggle between good and evil. In their play they reenact scenes from life; their play is a form of depiction. Naturally, they throw themselves into the battle against the forces of evil. Therefore they need weapons to play with — toy guns. The desire to play with guns need not in all cases be seen as a moral or spiritual fault that needs correcting. The children want to step into the hero's role — as leaders, policemen, soldiers. They also play at being doctors and fathers and mothers.

Some children, unfortunately, take pleasure in brutality and inflicting pain. However, the pain they inflict usually has little to do with toy guns. When they wish to hurt animals and other children, they can easily find makeshift weapons capable of causing real injury — or they resort to their bare hands.

V

The insight that play parallels and somehow recapitulates the struggle between good and evil in this world also has implications for adult life. Some thinkers have argued that the evil impulses in man can never be fully eliminated or trusted to remain dormant. We find such thinkers especially in the ranks of those who view evil as necessary (see Chapter 5 above). These thinkers take evil very seriously and argue that it cannot be fully divorced from our impulse to do good. In other words, the "demonic" can never be fully separated from the divine or angelic.

Lionel Rubinoff, a spokesman for this point of view, writes:

What if man's capacity for evil is an essential rather than an accidental or an acquired part of his nature? What if his very capacity to love and create depends upon how he "lives through" and assimilates his primordial urge to murder and destroy? What if good and evil, rather than being opposites, are in fact dialectical partners? . . . It is the transcendence of evil which concerns us here. And I am suggesting that it is only when man learns how to celebrate in and ritualize his primordial disposition to evil that he can transcend it. To transcend evil means to have first lived through it — which is why the history of man, what we learn from it, and how we live it over again, is so vitally important to man's future salvation.

The possibility of real virtue exists only for a man who has the freedom to choose evil. It is only for the man who has first "lived through" (imaginatively or otherwise) the choice of evil that the real meaning of virtue is disclosed for the first time. But the first stage in the dialectic of human redemption through the imaginative encounter with evil is learning to refuse all illusions: whether it be the illusion of man as an angel led astray by wicked forces from afar, or the illusion of man wholly driven by demonic forces from within. Man exists at the center of a contradiction which can be resolved only by "living through," in imagination and understanding, *all* of his intrinsic possibilities. It is only, to repeat, through the imaginative transcendence of evil that the future of mankind can be secured.[2]

I would take issue with Rubinoff on his theoretical understanding of evil, but it seems to me that his emphasis on squarely confronting the evil impulses within ourselves is sound. Evil exists not just in the hearts of certain people we call our enemies but in the heart of every one of us. The impulse to commit acts of hatred and destruction is a factor we must all cope with.

This recognition should serve as a corrective to the tendency to think in "good guys versus bad guys" terms. Although we need the Nazis as "bad guys," we must admit that there are certain impulses within *ourselves* which could easily develop in a Nazi direction. This admission, in turn, is in effect an affirmation that the original sin committed by Adam is really *our* sin. We, too, stand condemned and could well have done the same thing in his place.

The awareness that the opposition between good and evil is within our very hearts should lead to a mature appreciation of stories and art in which the line between good and evil is not so easy to discern. We live much of our lives in moral and religious ambiguity. Even though we delight in seeing the defeat of the Nazis reenacted in history and art and we celebrate their fall each time, we must also develop an eye for the complexities and ambiguities with which the people enmeshed in the Nazi system had to live. We must learn to recognize their sins and decisions and failures as utterly human, so that we will ultimately confess: "There, but for the grace and providence of God, go I."

The confrontation with art and historical narrative that forces us to peer into the abyss of evil threatening to swallow all humanity should teach us spiritual and moral humility. If we resist the depths of evil, it is not because evil has no hold on our hearts. Rather, we must join the psalmist in his praise of God: "He drew me up from the desolate pit, out of the miry bog, and set my feet upon a rock, making my steps secure" (Psalm 40:2).

The ancient notion of *catharsis* thus needs a Christian interpretation. In other words, there is an overcoming of evil possible through the depiction of evil in drama, art, and history. But the victory never consists in declaring evil unreal or isolating it in such a way as to keep it at a distance. Instead the catharsis or purgation of evil takes the form of a confession of sin (including an admission of universal human sinfulness) and an acceptance of God's forgiving and sustaining grace.

VI

The recognition of the enormous power of evil should also be our starting point when we return to the question of depicting sex. On the one hand there seems to be a need for restrictions here; unrestrained depictions of sexual acts can lead to serious problems. On the other hand, we cannot simply rule out any depiction of sex. In art and in narrative history, all sorts of sinful acts are depicted. It would seem that if the depiction of sex is somehow to be restricted, it cannot be solely on the grounds that it is sinful.

Perhaps we can better get at the question if we disregard sinful sex for the moment and pay no attention to promiscuity and sexual aberrations. Suppose we restrict ourselves to heterosexual intercourse between husband and wife. Is there anything wrong with depicting sex that takes place within the framework of marriage? Should intercourse between husband and wife be photographed and filmed?

The issue that comes up here is shame. Most husbands and wives would simply refuse to be photographed or filmed by outsiders. They would insist that their sexual relations are private, and that modesty is called for. They could even quote Augustine in their defense: ". . . no husband wants a single witness when he is rightfully doing his marital duty."[3] We are reminded of what we read in the Bible about the consequences of the fall into sin: "Then the eyes of both [Adam and Eve] were opened, and they knew they were naked; and they sewed fig leaves together and made themselves aprons" (Genesis 3:7).

VII

The question we must ask ourselves at this juncture is: How did the consequences of the fall into sin affect human sexuality? We might expect Augustine, as a thinker who made so much of lust and fought such an intense personal battle against sexual sin, to downplay the meaning of sex before the fall, but in fact he does no such thing. The purity of human life before the fall is not a purity achieved through sexual guardedness. In fact, Augustine is rather uninhibited in his view of sex before the fall:

> Had there been no fall, there would have been none of the embarrassment I now feel in pursuing this matter further, and no need to apologize for possible offense to chaste ears. On the contrary, one could feel free to discuss every detail connected with sex without the least fear of indelicacy. There would, in fact, be no such thing as an unbecoming word and no reference to one part of the body could be any more improper than reference to the other parts.[4]

Augustine suggests that before the fall people had their sexual impulses and desires under control in a way that sinful man today can only imagine:

> When we consider how many other human organs still obey the will even after the fall, we have no reason for doubting that the one unruly member could have done the same, so long as there was no defiance from lust. After all, we move our hands and feet to their appropriate functions whenever we choose and with no rebellion on their part. . . . Why, then, should we refuse to believe that the organs of generation, in the absence of that lust which is a just penalty imposed because of the sin of rebellion, could have obeyed men's wills as obediently as other organs do?[5]

Augustine seems to be pointing to sexuality as a weak spot in man. The "one unruly member" defies him and lust inflames him, sometimes without warning. How is man to keep his sexual impulses in check?

The answer seems to be twofold. First of all, there is shame and modesty connected with sex and the body after the fall. Second, the act of love becomes something to be done in private. Both these points, of course, are disputed by certain people in our time who tell us that there is no place for modesty and shame in connection with sex and who then go on to argue that sexual intercourse is just as appropriate in a party setting as in the privacy of the bedroom.

Why must sex remain private and hidden from the eyes of others? Primarily because it is capable of unleashing envy and jealousy and of stirring up feelings of insecurity. Openness in sexual practices would indeed be an incitement to lust (to use Augustine's term). When lovers seek privacy in order to make love, it is not solely because they prefer privacy but also out of deference to others: they are aware of the difficulties their love-making might lead to in the hearts and minds of other people.

The envy and insecurity of which I spoke are factors especially for adolescents, but they never fully disappear from the scene for adults either. The sight of an attractive nude or seminude body of the opposite sex is an incitement to lust for many people. And expressions of sexual affection, while not wrong in themselves, are sometimes hard for observers to cope with. Therefore we develop codes of propriety to govern such things. Lovers show themselves to each other only and display their sexual affection in private.

VIII

We saw earlier that Augustine did not seem to think there was shame before the fall into sin. Adam and Eve only became conscious of their nakedness afterward. Does this mean that we may speak of "shameless" sex before the fall?

In answer to this question I would say simply that shame does not enter the picture. Adam and Eve could apparently walk around unclothed without any sense of immodesty. Absolute privacy during sexual intercourse would presumably not have been necessary either: envy and lust were not lurking in the heart waiting to burst into flame.

But if "shameless" sex was all right *then*, why wouldn't it be all right *today*? I believe a text from Paul gives us the answer. Paul writes to the church in Corinth that although there is a sense in which "all things are lawful," it must be remembered that not all things are helpful and upbuilding. He elaborates as follows: "Let no one seek his own good, but the good of his neighbor" (I Corinthinans 10:23 — 24). The implication for our sexuality is clear: it may be that nudity and making love out in the open are "lawful" in principle, but they are surely not expedient. In order to avoid giving offense to others or leading them to sin, we must be modest in our dress and circumspect about our sexual displays of affection. Sexual love between husband and wife is not to be filmed or photographed to satisfy the curiosity of some third party. In this fallen world, sex seeks privacy.

IX

This is not to say that there is no place for the depiction of sex (including sinful sex) in art and historical narratives. If art and history are truly to deal with life, sex cannot be excluded. Still, the general rule to be followed is that sex should not so much be depicted as alluded to and imagined — or in some cases symbolized. A full sex life may be part of a drama, but the sex acts themselves could well occur offstage, like the murder in *Macbeth*.

To include explicit sex within art, drama, and historical narrative is to risk lapsing into pornography. It is not necessary to argue that an entire art work is either pornographic or it is not; individual scenes and incidents within an art work can be pornographic.

The term *pornography* is not so hard to define, although it is indeed difficult to use the definition as a criterion by means of which we can always determine whether a piece of art or narrative is or is not pornography. George P. Elliott offers the following definition: "Pornography is the representation of directly or indirectly erotic acts with an intrusive vividness which offends decency without aesthetic justification.."[6] The affront to decency must be understood as including incitement to lust and sexual waywardness.

I grant that the application of such a definition is open to disagreement, but the same is true of many other standards and norms. The extent to which pornography should be suppressed or banned by *law* is a question I leave to others. Suffice it to say that there are dangers involved in the censorship of pornography, as I already indicated in Chapter 9.

X

There yet remains the question of erotic art, which includes artistic depictions of nudes, art and literature that is sexually suggestive, and so forth. I believe it should be admitted first of all that the distinction between pornography and erotic art cannot always be clearly drawn. Still, it is important to hold out for a separate, legitimate category of erotic art.

The key to the distinction is to be found in Elliott's definition quoted above. Elliott speaks of representation or depiction "without aesthetic justification." This suggests that sexual explicitness is sometimes called for within the framework of an aesthetically worthwhile conception. Such artistic depiction might have the effect of arousing lust in some people, even though that was not the purpose. Modestly dressed women also arouse lust in some men.

It is not possible to spell out properly what erotic art is apart from a full-fledged theory of art. Since this is not the place for developing a theory of art, I will restrict myself to affirming that the human body, along with everything else in God's good creation, is a potential subject for artistic depiction.

Finally, there is the question whether there ought to be any restrictions on the viewing of erotic art. It seems to me unavoidable that there be some, however indirectly they might be implemented. There are erotic works of art that younger children probably should not view. If children can be restricted somewhat in what they see, artists will be able to develop erotic themes with less worry about the difficulties their art might cause.

No formal restrictions, however, should be necessary for adults. An adult who does not have the maturity and balance to view erotic art must impose some discipline on himself, recognizing that although all things are lawful, not all things are expedient.

PART FOUR
EVIL
AND
ESCHATOLOGY

IN one sense, making a statement on the problem of evil requires choosing between *theodicy* and *eschatology*. I have no theodicy to offer, no justification of God's decisions in the face of the evil in the world. Instead I believe we must look ahead to the coming triumph over evil, to the establishment of the Kingdom of God which is already among us but is not yet fully manifest and recognized.

In this interim age between Christ's first and second comings, the Kingdom of God is forcing its way into the world. The battle against evil is part of the coming of the Kingdom. One dimension of the battle is the phenomenon known as punishment. We also restrain evil by means of moral and religious education. In the final analysis, such education must aim at instilling an awareness of the types and dimensions of evil (Chapter 13).

The progress of God's Kingdom and the battle against evil are being hindered in our time by a certain outlook that is very influential in the modern world and that also affects many Christians — the liberal mind. All too often, this outlook minimizes or ignores the reality of evil. There are theoretical (i.e., theological and philosophical) reasons for this (Chapter 14).

As we explore the theme of learning to live with evil, we must recognize the reality of judgment as an aspect of the coming of the Kingdom. A theology that retreats from the prospect of divine judgment is likely to wind up in the clutches of the liberal mind. The road to Christ's return and the final victory of His Kingdom involves much struggle and pain (Chapter 15).

CHAPTER THIRTEEN

PUNISHMENT AND MORAL EDUCATION

I

PUNISHMENT is not a pleasant topic. Many people recoil from the very thought of punishment. Who, they ask, has the right to inflict pain or suffering on his fellow human beings? If we are committed to reducing evil, why not begin by eliminating punishment?

The only adequate answer to such a line of argument is that punishment comes into the world as a result of sin. Thus, if we are to talk sensibly about punishment, we must first talk about sin, recognizing that without sin there would be no need for punishment. Punishment is not part of God's grand design for man. James Orr writes:

> Sin, it has been seen, in its very nature, cuts the bond of fellowship with God, but, further, as entailing guilt, creates in man a feeling of alienation and distrust, and calls forth a reaction of the divine holiness against itself — what Scripture speaks of as the "wrath" (*orgé*) of God — which expresses itself in "judgment" (*krima*; "condemnation," *katakrima*), or punishment. The punishment of sin is no mere "fate," or "destiny," or impersonal, self-acting "law," without connexion with a moral Will, as in popular writing it is often represented, but has in and behind it the intensity of a divine righteousness. The truth to be firmly grasped here is, that this is no arbitrary relation of God to the sin of the world. It is grounded in His very nature, and cannot be laid aside by any act of will, any more than the moral law itself can be reversed or annulled. Sin is that against which the Holy One and Upholder of the moral order of the universe, *must* eternally declare Himself in judgment. To do otherwise would be to deny that He is God.[1]

Thus God punishes sin, and He authorizes human beings in certain roles (or offices) to do the same — parents, judges, teachers, and so forth.

When we speak of punishment, we should not try to disguise it as something pleasant, even though it is true that punishment is tied in with good purposes in some long-range way. Ernest van den Haag offers a straightforward definition of punishment as "a deprivation, or suffering, imposed by law."[2] Van den Haag speaks in the context of the punishment of criminals. For purposes of the discussion in this chapter, I would broaden the definition slightly to make it: deprivation or suffering imposed in response to wrong-doing by some person or agency authorized to do so.

It is generally recognized that there are two aspects to punishment: retribution (exacting a cost from the offender) and deterrence (discouraging future occurrences of the same offense). Which one is uppermost?

In Part II we saw that some thinkers (e.g., those who are influenced by the Platonist tradition) view natural evil as more basic than moral evil or sin. James Orr characterizes this position as "naturalistic" and contrasts it with the Christian position:

> While, however, in naturalistic systems moral evil is apt to fall behind natural evil, in Christianity it is the other way — the moral evil is throughout placed in the forefront, and natural evil is looked at mainly in the light of it. This is as it should be; for while, as we shall see, natural evil presents an independent problem, there can be no doubt that its existence is deeply implicated with the existence of moral evil.[3]

When the "naturalists" turn to the question of punishment, they usually make deterrence the primary purpose. Other thinkers (e.g., those who stand in the Calvinist tradition) instead make moral evil primary and understand punishment primarily in terms of retribution.

The contrast between these two traditions can be further elucidated as follows. The Platonist tradition tends to view man as good *by nature*: since evil is non-being, all that exists is good insofar as it exists. But man is also evil; that is to say, he is imperfect, lacking in certain respects, for he is not all that he might be. Hence we can also say that he is evil *by nature*, or evil by virtue of his very makeup. Earlier we noted that Augustine argued that it makes no sense to speak of the devil as sinful if he is evil *by nature* (see p. 58 above). The same point can be made with regard to man: if he is evil *by nature*, he cannot very well be called sinful and be held responsible for what he lacks.

The implications for the question of punishment are not hard to draw. If evil is rooted in our very *nature*, if we are evil simply by virtue of what we are (and are not), then retribution or punishment for shortcomings is surely out of place.

The Calvinist tradition, on the other hand, holds that man is evil *by choice*. In Adam all of mankind sinned freely. People who sin and commit crimes today are to be judged as free and responsible persons, even if they are not free to *reverse* completely their course in life. As they move freely down sin's slippery slope, they are *responsible* and accountable for their actions. Even the sinner bears the image of God in some sense.

II

Calvinism is not a stylish way of thinking today. Punishment is also out of fashion. In most modern Humanist thinking, natural evil is given primacy over moral evil. The response to so-called criminal behavior is then a policy aimed at deterrence. The offender must be deterred from repeating his offense, and other potential offenders must be deterred as well.

This outlook claims there is no place for punishment. The very concept of punishment, we are told, is a relic of an earlier, darker era. A. S. Neill, the founder of the famous Summerhill School in England, writes: "Punishment is hate. A woman who hits her child does not love that child. In the case of children, physical punishment is always cowardly; it's hitting someone who cannot hit back."[4] Thus in Neill's view, there is no room for corporal punishment in the home or the school. It has been argued that punishment is also inappropriate as a means of dealing with criminals. Arthur Lelyveld declares that "the concept of punishment has no place in enlightened criminology."[5]

If punishment is to be abolished, what will take its place? Rehabilitation, we are told. But is there really a significant difference between the two? John Delaney observes: ". . . the dichotomy between punishment and rehabilitation is illusory. All forms of limitation upon freedom and self-determination constitute punishment from the standpoint of the offender."[6]

The defenders of rehabilitation, however, like to contrast

"vindictive punishment" with "enlightened treatment." Harry Elmer Barnes explains why:

> In the first place, our modern knowledge of the nature of criminal conduct renders the whole conception of punishment archaic. It is as futile and foolish to punish a criminal as it is to punish a person suffering from a physical or mental disease. In the second place, it is not the crime which needs to be dealt with, but the criminal. Hence, modern criminology supplants the old slogan of making the punishment fit the crime by the new objective of making the treatment fit the criminal. If we accept this view of the matter, it becomes clear that the treatment must be carried out by those competent in the premises: obviously, physiologists, physicians, psychiatrists and sociologists, but not lawyers, except in so far as they are . . . criminologists. The diagnosis and treatment of the criminal is a highly technical medical and sociological problem for which the lawyer is rarely any better fitted than a real estate agent or a plumber. We shall ultimately come to admit that society has been as unfortunate in handing over criminals to lawyers and judges in the past as it once was in entrusting medicine to shamans and astrologers, and surgery to barbers.[7]

Here we have the illness metaphor again (see p. 65 above). Crime becomes a technical problem; adjustments must be made by professionals and experts. Particularly significant is the statement that we deal not with the *crime* but with the *criminal.* The actual evil (i.e., the criminal deed) is disregarded, and the doer undergoes adjustment like an automobile in need of a tune-up.

Barnes is well aware that this view of crime has a theoretical basis without which it cannot be properly understood or defended. What it presupposes is a certain view of man, a view that strips man of freedom and responsibility:

> As soon as the public comes to regard crime as a socio-medical problem, we shall have little trouble in getting general consent to hand over its treatment to psychiatrists and sociologists.
>
> The greatest obstacle to successful public education on this point resides in the popular theologico-metaphysical conception of man as a free moral agent, capable of arbitrary self-determination of conduct irrespective of physical ancestry or social experience. We must educate the public to accept the scientific view of the socio-biological determination of conduct, which at once undermines the whole basis of the conventional theory of punishment and opens the way for the socio-medical treatment of the person who commits an anti-social act. We must not, however, underestimate the difficulty which we shall meet in uprooting the archaic free-moral-agent conception.[8]

III

Because natural evil is regarded as basic and primary in this view, the disease or illness metaphor is used extensively. Indeed, it ceases to function as a metaphor in the strict sense. Frank Pakenham (Lord Longford), writing from a Catholic standpoint, objects to such thinking: "But the vast majority of crimes are sins and if, in fact, we were going to excuse them as simply manifestations of disease we should be well on the way to rejecting altogether the attempt to distinguish between good conduct and bad."[9]

There is much more to be said in criticism of the view of punishment as treatment or therapy. Isn't there something demeaning and degrading about compulsory "treatment" that disregards crime and relies on whatever behavior modification techniques the social sciences may be able to provide in order to alter future behavior to specifications set by the professionals and experts? And if the crime is to be disregarded, how do we decide who the criminals (i.e., the candidates for treatment and rehabilitation) are?

These are weighty issues. Gerrit Brillenburg Wurth, who deals with punishment from a Calvinistic point of view, observes that God shows man a certain honor or respect when He punishes him; that is to say, He regards him as responsible, accountable for what he has done.[10] The philosopher Hegel made a similar point in arguing that when a criminal is punished, "he is honoured as a rational being." Hence Hegel warned against the notion that a criminal can be "treated either as a harmful animal who has to be made harmless, or with a view to deterring and reforming him."[11] The needed change ought to come from within.

In the language of law a comparable point can be made in terms of civil rights. H. B. Acton argues: "There is something incongruous about a free society's regarding all breakers of the law as sick men and treating them as patients."[12] Ernest van den Haag points to the same problem when he contrasts the "justice model" with the "therapeutic model":

> In the justice model the convict, punished according to desert, leaves when he has served his time, as legally prescribed for the crime for which he was convicted. He does not depend on the approval or disapproval of his jailers. The correctional or therapeutic model implies that he will leave when his needs have been met. The needs, however,

are not those he feels but those he is felt to have. Experts and prison authorities decide on them, and on the length of his stay. The "needs" they attribute to the convict derive from their own notions about proper behavior and lifestyle. . . . If he is held because bad behavior is predicted, he is, as it were, made to suffer in advance for his expected future acts.[13]

If such methods of dealing with criminals are adopted in our society, will freedom survive the reign of the experts who correct our behavior and take us off the street for further treatment and adjustment if they have reason to believe we might engage in acts that are not approved of? How does such a policy regarding "crime" differ essentially from what goes on in the Soviet Union, where dissenters are detained and "treated" in mental hospitals? Who is to decide whether behavior of a certain sort is desirable or undesirable? Is this a question of law, or must we leave it to the social scientists?

IV

As we turn from criminology to education, we find significant parallels. Both the criminologist and the educator (at least in part) are in the business of fighting evil and dealing with offenders and wrongdoers. Moreover, both are in the business of prevention. The criminologist, it has been suggested, concerns himself not so much with crime as with the criminal. His aim is to instill an acceptable pattern of behavior in the convicted criminal in his custody. The educator also aims at behavioral results — not just in the classroom but in later life. Many educators regard behavioral results as the central objective in moral or religious education.

Criminology relies heavily on the social sciences as it does battle with evil, and so does modern religious education. James Michael Lee, a Catholic educational theorist, is a leading exponent of the "social-science approach" to religious education: "Riding in the social-science rocket, religious instruction can break out of the gravitational pull of past failures." What is the overall aim? Lee speaks of "the effective incarnation of theology within the lifestyle of learners."[14]

Lee explains his position at length and in detail. He writes: ". . . the religion teacher fundamentally is a professional specialist in the modification of student behavior as it affects his religious life."[15] This involves spelling out carefully just what Christian living or Christian behavior consists of: "If religious instruction is to successfully accomplish its task of facilitating Christian living, then it is absolutely imperative that Christian living be defined operationally. Which specific behaviors and bundles of behaviors go to form Christian living?"[16]

Lee identifies these as the questions that must be faced squarely when a curriculum for religious instruction is drawn up. He writes:

> The objectives of future religion curricula should be stated in behavioral, performance terms. . . . A curriculum, if it is to be teachable, should specify which behaviors are involved in growing in love for God. It should spell out the behaviors which constitute a "real" understanding of the consequences of sin. These behaviors should be expressed in observable performance terms, namely, that level of performance the learner must demonstrate to himself and to the teacher to indicate that he has indeed learned the behavior involved.[17]

Lee distinguishes his approach from behaviorism, calling it "behavioralism" instead. The latter is broader than the former, he explains: "All behaviorists are behavioralists, but not all behavioralists are behaviorists."[18]

At this point one might wonder what becomes of the *content* of religious education. Doesn't Christian education have something to do with teaching Christian doctrine? Lee assures us that it does, explaining that his approach transforms theological content into religious behavior:

> The religion curriculum of the future should revolve around the teaching of Christian doctrine. However, it is of paramount importance to note that Christian doctrine is not, nor can it ever be, simply limited to the cognitive content of Christianity. Such a stricture would be a cruel twisting and distortion of everything Jesus stood for and taught. Christian doctrine is an operationalized pattern of life. Christian doctrine in its authentic form is Christian living. Christian doctrine is a lifestyle. . . . The goal of religious instruction in the future ought not so much to be the production of Christian thinkers as of Christian doers. The development of Christian thinkers should remain the task of Christian graduate schools.[19]

Since the emphasis is placed on Christian "doing," many of the barriers to ecumenical cooperation fall away. Lee writes: ". . . I hope to inaugurate a trend toward a truly ecumenical approach to religious education at every level, theoretical and practical."[20] How is this possible? We are speaking here of a *method*, as Lee explains: "The social-science approach to religious instruction is value-free in terms of any and all specific theological positions. It can accommodate a Pelagian, an Augustinian, a Thomist, a Jansenist, or an advocate of the new theology."[21]

V

Lee's approach to religious education is based on the conviction that specified teacher initiatives will lead to predictible student learning or "behaviors." He explains that there is an

> empirically demonstrated causal relationship between the teacher's antecedant pedagogical behaviors and the student's consequent performance behaviors. From teaching theory it is possible to devise and design prescriptive and predictive statements about effective educational practice. The content and contours of the teaching theory are derived from hard empirical research data on the dynamics of the facilitational act and the learning process.[22]

If the correlation is so precise, if teaching is indeed a technical activity, it is surely a job for trained professionals. Indeed, professionalism is the key, Lee tells us: "All religion teachers should hold a master's degree in religious instruction." Upper-echelon administration, he goes on, requires a doctorate.[23]

So exact is the new science of religious education that we can even think in terms of a student's RQ (religious quotient). Lee explains: "IQ simply indicates a person's mental ability, while RQ indicates his ability specifically with respect to religious values."[24]

There is a certain amount of technical jargon involved in Lee's theory of religious education, but the essence of his position is not so hard to state. The emphasis falls on Christian *doing* rather than Christian thinking or comprehension or discernment. Lifestyle or observable conduct is the key. Lee writes:

> Religious behaviors are not some sort of vague, amorphous, spooky phenomena, but rather an identifiable set of behaviors. If religious behaviors were not identifiable, then how would it be possible for religious educators or churchmen or theologians to be able to identify the religious person or the just man? Can we not observe the difference between a religious man and a sinful man by his cognitive, affective, and lifestyle behaviors? To be sure, the whole notion and meaning of sin are wiped out when one insists that it is impossible to identify and

assess the quality of an individual's behaviors. "You will be able to tell them by their fruits" (Matthew 7:16), that is by their behaviors.[25]

VI

In Protestant circles we find a similar shift from the traditional emphasis on Christian thinking and understanding to Christian *doing* or activity. In a recent book significantly entitled *Educating for Responsible Action*, Nicholas Wolterstorff offers the notion of "tendency learning" as basic to defining objectives in education. He tells us that Christian education must concern itself with "cultivating the appropriate *tendencies* in the child. It will have tendency learning as one of its fundamental goals."[26]

Wolterstorff claims to see inadequacies in Christian education as it has been understood in his own tradition:

> It used to be said, particularly in the Calvinist tradition, that the goal of Christian education is to impart to the student the Christian "world and life view." The intent behind putting it this way was to affirm that the gospel pertains to all of life and not just to some "religious" part. But this formulation is inadequate, for it puts too much emphasis on a "view," that is, on what we have called cognition. To be identified with the people of God and to share in its work does indeed require that one have a system of belief — call it "the Christian world and life view." But it requires more than that. It requires the Christian *way of life*. Christian education is education aimed at training for the Christian way of life, not just education aimed at inculcating the Christian world and life view.[27]

Wolterstorff focuses primarily on moral education, but he does not rule out "tendency learning" for other areas: ". . . the lessons learned in moral education can be applied to other tendency learning." The areas he mentions by way of example are the political, aesthetic, artistic, recreational, economic, and ecological domains.[28] Thus his theory has broad implications for objective setting: "Education must aim at producing alterations in what students tend (are disposed, are inclined) to do. It must aim at tendency learning."[29]

It is significant that Wolterstorff, like Lee, claims ecumenical application and relevance for his theory: ". . . it is as relevant to other traditions of Christianity as to the Calvinist. Indeed, in the central part of the book, we offer a perspective applicable to education generally, not just to Christian education."[30]

VII

It is in the context of the theme of learning to live with evil that I have brought up for discussion some recent theories of education and criminal behavior. It seems to me that something is missing in these theories: they tend to disregard the evil act and impulse in their eagerness to cultivate what is good. I believe that in the long run, correction and education which seeks to replace the evil act with the good act will run stuck — in the case of a great many individuals, at least. Evil is not a gap or a hole to be filled, something negative which disappears or ceases to be a factor when something positive comes along.

I do believe there is a place for tendency learning and the setting of educational objectives in terms of acquired skills and desired conduct. But I am also convinced that much of the significant impact of education is mysterious and incalculable. In this regard education is somewhat like preaching: the preacher who sows the good seed of God's Word can never be sure what the harvest will be or when it will be gathered in. It is God who gives the growth. James D. Smart therefore sounds a timely warning:

> It is this mystery in the making of a Christian that the religious educator is inclined to forget. He begins to think that he has a technique by which the desired result can be secured. He can do it by education. But if the desired result is really the making of a Christian . . . the claim is that education can control and produce a development in human beings that, according to the New Testament, is the work of the Holy Spirit through the gospel of Jesus Christ. But to claim to do what only God can do is blasphemy![31]

We must recognize a clear distinction, then, between education and conversion. There is indeed a place for "tendency learning" and the correction in which the criminologist engages, provided we bear in mind that these are lower level forms of learning. Small children need to learn tendencies long before they understand the reason why. They must be made to keep off the busy street in front of the house regardless of whether they understand the danger. Some criminals may have to be psychically pressured to stay away from certain forms of reprehensible behavior without fully knowing and accepting that the behavior in question is wrong. But the *goal* of education is always something much higher — the molding of a way of life that is rooted in a "world and life view." In short, education must lead to spiritual discernment, to genuine Biblical wisdom.

Such spiritual discernment is ultimately a knowledge of good and evil, and such knowledge is in turn impossible apart from thought and reflection. The inculcation of appropriate behavior patterns is no substitute for teaching students how the clash between good and evil in this world is ultimately to be understood, namely, as the cosmic warfare between Christ and Satan. In the words of Lord's Day 1 of the Heidelberg Catechism, I need to learn about evil so that I will know "how great my sin and misery are" and "how I am set free from all my sins and misery." In other words, I need to know something about the dimensions of evil (see Chapter 8 above).

Once we recognize that such a knowledge of good and evil *must* come into the picture, we see that religious education can only be *Christian* education rooted in the Bible. It is not education compatible with any and every theological position, and its procedure cannot simply be incorporated into the curriculum in secular schools.

This is only another way of saying that religious education needs an eschatological framework. In the face of evil, students must be taught the significance of Christ's final victory over evil and death: "I have the keys of Death and Hades" (Revelation 1:18). The ultimate issue in religious education is not appropriate tendencies or behaviors but a choice for or against Christ, the leader of the forces of good. That choice must be made freely and cannot be predicted.

The same perspective can be applied to the question of the punishment of criminals. The criminal is still a human being bearing God's image. When he commits a crime, his punishment must be understood first of all as retribution. Once he has served his sentence (and provided he has the mental capacity to choose *not* to commit further crimes), he has the *right* to go free and may not be detained simply because he is capable of more crime. We are all capable of sin and crime.

This is not to say that there is no place for rehabilitation in prison. Some convicts do change their ways — all too few, unfortunately. But *genuine* rehabilitation requires building on a firm foundation; it requires the perspective of the coming Kingdom. Rehabilitation is not simply the replacement of less desirable behavior patterns by more desirable ones. True rehabilitation of one's life calls for spiritual discernment, a recognition of what evil really is — rebellion against God and the alienation and judgment it entails.

The change that is called for goes beyond outward behavior; it is a change in the heart. In rehabilitation as in education and preaching, there are mysterious, incalculable factors at work. We must never forget that our God moves in a mysterious way.

CHAPTER FOURTEEN

THE
LIBERAL
MIND

I

IN this chapter I will examine the liberal mind and its approach to dealing with evil. In using the term *liberalism*, I do not mean to refer to the whole range of ways of thinking to which this term is generally applied. In particular, I do not mean to discuss the various modern theologies that find inspiration in either Hegel or Schleiermacher, even though these theologies are often characterized as "liberal."

In Chapter 5 I dealt briefly with the conception of evil as necessary, which we find in both Hegel and Schleiermacher. In the final analysis, this conception accords evil too much status: evil, we are told, is necessary in order for good to be (or become) what it is. Thus it cannot be denied that this tradition takes evil seriously as a factor to be reckoned with. It surely does not minimize evil.

The liberal tradition I mean to discuss in this chapter has its roots in Platonism (or Neoplatonism) and the view of evil as non-being (see Chapter 6 above). Generally speaking, this tradition is heavily represented in Great Britain and North America, whereas the view of evil as necessary is influential especially in continental Europe. The overall criticism I shall raise is that the liberal tradition in the Anglo-American world does not take evil seriously enough. This is a failing first of all on the theoretical level, but it has practical and existential consequences as well.

II

Because it is infected with a superficial optimism, the liberal mind does not give us much guidance in the face of the world's evil. James Burnham writes that the liberal ideology, "by clinging to an optimistic theory of human nature and history, by denying the objective reality of evil and affirming that all social problems can be solved, excludes genuine tragedy."[1] The reason liberalism offers little concrete advice in coping with evil is that it does not see evil as a genuine threat. Ronald Butts observes: ". . . the liberal lives by a sort of inverted Gresham's law which assumes that the good cannot possibly be driven out by the bad."[2]

This liberal outlook does make some sense when considered on its own terms. If evil is indeed non-being, how could it ever displace the good, which has the status of something that exists positively? It would seem that the positive approach must always win out in the end. Evil is essentially a vacuum, an empty space that needs to be filled with something positive, something good.

The liberal, then, is optimistic about the progress being made in the battle between good and evil. J. Gresham Machen writes: "A cardinal doctrine of modern liberalism is that the world's evil may be overcome by the world's good; no help is thought to be needed from outside the world."[3] Hence the liberal manifests little interest in an eschatalogical outlook in which the final victory over the forces of evil is won by a transcendent power that interrupts human history and brings it to a consummation.

III

Liberalism is not a casually held set of beliefs. Salvador de Madariaga, who describes himself as a "born liberal," observes: ". . . one is born liberal as one is born blond or brunette." What he means by this is that liberalism is at bottom an attitude, a temperament.[4]

Liberalism is not strong on principles but characteristically manifests a surprising degree of openness to all sorts of strange views. Madariaga points to

a certain neutrality in regard to the opinions of others. The liberal will thus have a tendency to react by a "Maybe you're right" at the assertion of the most monstrous heresies. . . .

It is this intellectual hospitality to all comers which tends to make of liberalism an open house where the most badly assorted travelers may run into each other as in a huge caravansery. As a result of flinging open all doors to their widest, liberalism ends by having no more walls, by losing, in short, the very boundaries which should define it.[5]

This openness to all sorts of ways of thinking is tied in with liberalism's view of evil, which in turn has consequences for its understanding of truth. If evil, as the opposite of goodness, is non-being, then the opposite of truth must be non-knowledge. As non-knowledge, error does not pose a great threat but can easily be pushed aside when something positive comes along, namely, the truth. Madariaga therefore observes that for the liberal, error is simply a step on the way to knowledge.[6]

IV

There is, however, a definite theoretical structure to the liberalism that has its roots in Neoplatonism and its pantheist leanings. A system that believes that God is in all things or that all things find their unity in God, might be described as a "monistic" conception of reality. In a discussion of the "essence of liberalism," Kenneth Cauthen writes: "Reality is fundamentally one realm, one process, one structure of activities. There is continuity between the world and God and between nature and man. God is thought of as the Immanent Spirit or as the Purposive Power at work within nature and history."[7]

This notion of continuity is the major defining principle of the liberal mind. Cauthen explains how this theme is put to work in liberal thought.

> This theme manifests itself in every area of thought and permeates all liberal theology. There is practically no end to its application. It reduces the distinction between animals and men, men and God, nature and God, reason and revelation, Christ and other men, Christianity and other religions, nature and grace, the saved and the lost, justification and sanctification, Christianity and culture, the church and the world, the sacred and the secular, the individual and society, life here and hereafter, heaven and hell, the natural and the supernatural, the human and divine natures of Christ, etc.[8]

J. Gresham Machen presents a similar analysis of the liberal way of thinking. In his effort to set out the fundamental differences between liberalism and orthodox Christianity, he takes up the key question of the relation between Creator and creature:

Liberalism has lost sight of the very centre and core of the Christian teaching. In the Christian view of God as set forth in the Bible, there are many elements. But one attribute of God is absolutely fundamental in the Bible; one attribute is absolutely necessary in order to render intelligible all the rest. That attribute is the awful transcendence of God. From beginning to end the Bible is concerned to set forth the awful gulf that separates the creature from the Creator. It is true, indeed, that according to the Bible God is immanent in the world. Not a sparrow falls to the ground without Him. But He is immanent in the world not because He is identified with the world, but because He is the free Creator and Upholder of it. Between the creature and the Creator a great gulf is fixed.[9]

Machen believes that liberalism has succumbed to the pantheist temptation (see pp. 55–56 above). To use Cauthen's language, there is "continuity" between God and man, a continuity from which sin cannot be excluded in the final analysis. Machen writes:

In modern liberalism, on the other hand, this sharp distinction between God and the world is broken down, and the name "God" is applied to the mighty world process itself. . . . And modern liberalism, even when it is not consistently pantheistic, is at any rate pantheizing. It tends everywhere to break down the separateness between God and the world, and the sharp personal distinction between God and man. Even the sin of man on this view ought logically to be regarded as part of the life of God.[10]

When Creator and creature are joined together, all ideas of moral evil or sin as rebellion against the divine will and command must be eliminated. Sin can be no more than imperfection or finitude — an inevitable consequence of man's current situation as a being on the way to a brighter future. Machen contrasts the liberal position with orthodox Christianity:

Modern liberalism has lost all sense of the gulf that separates the creature from the Creator; its doctrine of man follows naturally from its doctrine of God. But it is not only the creature limitations of mankind which are denied. Even more important is another difference. According to the Bible, man is a sinner under the just condemnation of God; according to modern liberalism, there is really no such thing as sin. At the very root of the modern liberal movement is the loss of the consciousness of sin.[11]

V

In his critique of liberalism, Machen is careful to draw the consequences. He does not simply present liberalism as a version of the Christian faith with which he happens to disagree; for Machen, liberalism is not a species of Christianity at all. And if it is a type of religion, it is nonredemptive in character.[12] How could it be otherwise if there is no real consciousness of sin and the need for redemption?

But what is liberalism, then, if not an alternative doctrine of salvation? Liberalism clings to Christian terminology and claims to be a restatement of Christianity. Machen explains: "The liberal believes that applied Christianity is all there is of Christianity, Christianity being merely a way of life."[13]

Liberalism does not deny that many of the Christian creeds conflict with one another. But we saw earlier that liberalism throws its doors wide open, and that intellectual caravans originating in many different places find hospitality under its roof. Here the thesis that Christianity is essentially a way of life offers a significant perspective. Kenneth Minogue declares that the liberal mind responds to the conflicts between the creeds with

> an attempt to deny the importance of differences. All the creeds, it has been argued, contain a common core of reverence, worship and sociability: that is what is most important in religion. The rest is merely local variation. Why come to blows about transubstantiation or the immaculate conception? Doctrines of the Trinity are matters for theologians, not for ordinary men. In the seventeenth century, Spinoza argued that the essence of religion was in good works and good behaviour. Teaching a man religion was thus teaching him good behaviour: in other words, no more than a way of manipulating him.[14]

When liberalism begins to penetrate an orthodox denomination, certain signs become apparent. Doctrine and "worldview" receive less emphasis, and liturgy takes central stage. The sacraments, as activities, are given more weight, and the preaching of God's Word declines; the church often conforms to a "high church" model.

The notion that Christianity is essentially a way of life manifests itself in such churches in the form of Christian activism. Arguments are presented to the effect that evangelism means social and political involvement. The gospel is not an answer to the question "What must I do to be saved?" but a social and political program for the betterment of society as a whole.

VI

Liberalism's view of evil makes its presence felt in the liberal conception of man and society. The doctrine of original sin is, of course, also reformulated. J. Salwyn Schapiro neatly expresses the liberal conception of original sin: "Man, according to liberalism, is born ignorant, not wicked."[15]

Knowledge is good by definition and tends to increase human happiness — hence the liberal reluctance to tolerate any restraints on the flow of information through a free society. This has the effect of fostering the tradition of a free press, but it also has something to do with the assault on privacy in our time. Moreover, it leads to an increase in the amount of pornography in conspicuous circulation — especially pornography disguised as science (see pp. 81–82 above).

The church becomes a social agency and a political base of operations for liberalism. Yet the need for worship is not altogether overcome. Liberalism worships in a different temple; as James Burnham has pointed out, the *school* is liberalism's church.[16] Knowledge epitomizes goodness.

The school is viewed first and foremost as an institution for the fostering and transmission of scientific knowledge. Science is held in high esteem as the best guarantee of a bright future. Only in recent years have doubts about the wisdom of certain scientific research programs (e.g., nuclear energy, genetic engineering) begun to cause fundamental doubts about science among liberals.

The alliance between liberalism and science is still in effect. As we saw in the previous chapter, the social sciences are asked to supply up-to-date approaches and methods for all sorts of human problems, such as teaching children to do what's right and encouraging criminals to live within the bounds of the law. Knowledge and education are glorified in liberal circles; to lack a college or university degree is a serious deprivation. The spiritual dimension in knowledge and education is all but forgotten.

VII

Because liberalism believes that good triumphs over evil automatically, it does little to provide measures by which evil can be actively combated. The notion of punishment is regarded as objectionable. Since almost any exercise of power or coercion becomes problematic, ways have to be found to disguise coercion and punishment as forms of benevolence. Punishment therefore becomes rehabilitation.

Because of its tendency toward neutrality in disputes, liberalism generally shrinks from the application of standards to determine what's right and what's wrong. Its morality is comprised largely of sentiment or feelings of benevolence rather than rules and principles. Old-fashioned morality is condemned as unsuited to our time. Kenneth Minogue observes: ". . . the liberal objection to morality can be summed up in the formula: morality condemns, liberalism tries to understand."[17]

This pattern also carries over into politics on the national level, where we find liberalism tending to retreat from the exercise of power. There is a great uneasiness about maintaining military forces for purposes of national defence; hence liberals are often found arguing for disarmament proposals — even unilateral disarmament. They make a virtue of "vulnerability" as they exhort us to put our trust in God rather than weapons. They may need to be reminded that when Jesus was challenged by Satan to throw Himself off the temple since God would surely send angels to catch Him, He refused and said: "You shall not tempt the Lord your God" (Matthew 4:5–7).

The liberals who advocate unilateral disarmament, however, are not usually looking for intervention from angels. They simply cannot believe that an approach of openness and benevolence toward those who are perceived as the country's enemies will not overcome whatever enmity and disputes there might be.

In summary, then, liberalism does not have a great deal to say about learning to live with evil and combating evil, for it believes that evil can be eliminated gradually in the normal course of doing and promoting what is good. It sees no need for a crusade against evil.

CHAPTER FIFTEEN

JUDGMENT AND THE COMING KINGDOM

I

IT is not my intention to present Calvinism as the solution to the problem of evil. I do not believe that those who seek a theodicy or a theoretical solution to the problem will find it in Calvinism — or anywhere else, for that matter. What Calvinism offers instead is a perspective which does not dispel the mystery of evil but does indeed assist us in learning to cope with evil.

That perspective on evil cannot be divorced from an awareness of the coming Kingdom of God. The victory and full establishment of that Kingdom will spell the end for evil. Thus Calvinism responds to the problem of evil with an eschatology rather than a theodicy.

At the center of Calvinistic thought stands the theme of the sovereignty of God. Modern Humanism undertakes nothing less than a revolution when it replaces the sovereignty of God with the sovereignty of man. Liberal Christianity seeks a compromise between these two positions.

The Calvinist perspective on evil offers comfort and hope only if it is approached against the background of a prior commitment to the sovereignty of God. Those who presuppose the sovereignty of man and then set out to determine what Calvinism has to offer by way of a response to the problem of evil will inevitably be disappointed.

II

In the popular mind Calvinism is often associated with an ascetic morality, an austere way of life. It is true that Calvinists generally favor a sober approach to the affairs of this world, but asceticism and restraint do not *define* Calvinism. The central doctrine is the sovereignty of God, not a set of moral restraints.

The popular mind also associates *Puritanism* with Calvinism. There is indeed a connection between the two, although they should not be equated; not all Calvinists stand in the Puritan tradition. Still, the history of Puritan Calvinism in New England is a subject that deserves our reflection.

We saw earlier that the abandonment of Puritan Calvinism had something to do with the "ethicizing" of theology (see p. 74 above). The New England development in the direction of Arminianism and eventually Unitarianism cannot be understood apart from this "ethicizing" tendency on the part of those who lost sight of the meaning of God's sovereignty. Conrad Wright observes:

> The New England liberals were called Arminians, not because they were influenced directly by Jacobus Arminius (1560—1609), the Dutch Remonstrant, but because their reaction against Calvinism was similar to his.
>
> The Arminianism that Cotton Mather dismissed and Jonathan Edwards feared was the first phase of the liberal movement in theology which in the nineteenth century was named Unitarianism. It rejected the awful and inscrutable Deity of the Calvinists, and replaced him with a God of benevolence and law. It rejected the concept of human nature as totally corrupt and depraved, and supplanted it with one in which the ability of every man to strive for righteousness was admitted. It was, in a sense, the New England version of the theology of the Age of Reason, occupying a middle ground between orthodoxy on the one hand and infidelity on the other.[1]

The development sketched by Wright illustrates a point of the greatest importance: changes in the conception of God lead to changes in all aspects of theology. Once the Calvinists ceased to understand the relation between divine love and divine justice, once they began to think and talk in terms of an "inscrutable Deity" on whom one could not depend, the journey in the direction of Humanism (i.e., the sovereignty of man) by way of Arminianism, universalism, and Unitarianism became inevitable (see p. 75 above).

III

The New England rejection of God's sovereignty and justice is not an isolated incident. We find parallels to it elsewhere in the history of Christian thought. When an Augustinian conception of grace comes face to face with thinking inspired by Neoplatonism, conflict is inevitable.

A. H. Armstrong and R. A. Markus point out that although "Augustine could see in Platonism both a great liberating force and a means of achieving intellectual insight," in the end he often had to "repudiate it in the name of Christianity"[2] (see p. 58 above). But Armstrong does not draw the conclusion that one must side with Augustine against the Platonists. Elsewhere he complains that Augustine's "pessimism about man" becomes a "pessimism about God." The Augustinian doctrine of predestination presents the gospel as "very bad news, not good news." Armstrong therefore proposes to base his conception of God on Plato and the Platonists instead (see p. 53 above). He writes:

> The belief that the divine powers which rule the universe are perfectly good is the fundamental tenet of the religion of Plato and his successors. And being good for Plato and the Platonists means doing good, and doing it with perfect wisdom and fairness. To theists of this sort, and to many Christian Platonists who have been led on by the revelation in Jesus Christ from their Platonic belief that God is good to believe that he is Love, and who understand this as meaning more, not less, goodness than Plato or any philosopher was able to conceive, the doctrine of Augustine is intolerable, and no appeal to mystery can justify it. This rejection of any form of Augustinian selective predestination has, I think, been particularly characteristic of the English non-Calvinist and anti-Calvinist Christian tradition, which has, at times, been very deeply influenced by Platonism.[3]

IV

These "ethicizing" arguments against the doctrine of predestination occur at various points in the history of Christianity. They proceed from the standpoint of the sovereignty of man. Once man is made sovereign, there is no standard outside him by which he could be judged totally depraved and deserving of condemnation. Condemnation is therefore viewed as unfair. Such, in brief, is the so-called moral argument against Calvinism.

This argument was given a classic formulation early in the nineteenth century by William Ellery Channing. The problem with Calvinism, Channing declared, is ". . . the inconsistency of the system with the divine perfections. It is plain that a doctrine which contradicts our best ideas of goodness and justice cannot come from the just and good God, or be a true representation of his character." Are we then to put our own reasoning about God ahead of His revelation about Himself? Channing declares simply: ". . . the ultimate reliance of a human being is and must be on his own mind."[4]

Channing maintains that the consequences of the moral argument against Calvinism take time to sink in. There are many who still call themselves Calvinists but have broken with the essentials of Calvin's thought. Channing notes: "They keep the name, and drop the principles which it signifies. They adhere to the system as a whole, but shrink from all its parts and distinguishing points." Channing tells us that in his time there was a "silent but real defection from Calvinism" underway.[5]

V

Channing lived roughly a century after the great Calvinist theologian and philosopher Jonathan Edwards (1703 – 1758). Edwards is widely regarded as an extremist, as the preacher of damnation who warned people about the fate of "sinners in the hands of an angry God." It would be more accurate, however, to view him as a defender of an embattled Calvinism whose foundations were being eroded. The fact of the matter is that Edwards appeared on the scene relatively late in the history of New England Calvinism.

It is often assumed that Harvard University, founded in 1636, was a bastion of Calvinist orthodoxy in its earlier years. This is not entirely correct. Samuel Eliot Morison informs us that John Harvard, the clergyman whose library and estate gave the university its start, "had more volumes in his library by St. Thomas Aquinas than by St. John [Calvin] of Geneva." The New England Puritans were not all predestinarian Calvinists.[6] Elsewhere Morison writes: ". . . New England orthodoxy in the seventeenth century was not pure Calvinism. The English puritan divines in greatest repute in New England . . . had begun to explain away the rigors of predestination before Harvard was founded. . . ."[7]

The work of Edwards should be viewed not as a final statement of a venerable American Puritan Calvinism but as a fresh and somewhat original theological endeavor. And in its originality we also find its weakness and the key to its inability to arrest the Calvinist decline. Douglas J. Elwood points to the element of novelty in Edwards: "There is a noticeable difference in philosophical orientation between the Calvinism of Calvin and the neo-Calvinism of Edwards. The difference is not creedal but one of emphasis due to a different philosophical background." And what was the philosophical background which Edwards brought to his theology? Elwood writes that Edwards was "under the inspiration of Neoplatonism." His "overarching concern was to reconstruct the framework of historic Calvinism along Neoplatonic lines."[8] Roland André Delattre, in a book on the ethics and aesthetics of Edwards, points to "the tradition of Christian Platonism, to which Edwards is partly and quite consciously heir."[9]

Was Edwards a Platonist in the sense that he steeped himself in the Platonist tradition and looked to it for inspiration? Not necessarily. The Platonist strand in his thought might have come as a mere flash of light, perhaps during his days as a student at Yale, when a library of the latest philosophical writings came over from England, including some of the works of the Cambridge Platonists, a group of seventeenth-century English thinkers. A. C. McGiffert, Jr. suggests that the link between Edwards and the Platonist tradition was indeed somewhat remote:

> Throughout the course of European culture the mind of Plato has acted as a vital germ of influence, a constant ferment. The Platonic tradition . . . has persisted as a prominent feature of the spiritual landscape of Europe and America. Occasionally the Hellenic note seems to have been struck quite spontaneously, as though an individual had himself hit upon the same golden seam of insight that Plato had earlier discovered and exhibited to the world in golden words. Oftener, perhaps, the Greek interpretation of life has passed from mind to mind and from generation to generation like the fiery Greek beacons which carried from mountain top to mountain top the news that Troy had fallen, one enlightened spirit setting another on fire. So Shaftesbury or Cudworth or Hutcheson lit the mind of Edwards.[10]

VI

The effort made by Edwards to combine Platonism and Calvinism did not prove successful. In the final analysis, the two are not compatible. Calvinism proceeds from the sovereignty of God and establishes an ontological gulf that cannot be bridged between the Creator and the creature. Platonism, on the other hand, has strong pantheizing tendencies and tries to establish continuity between the being of man and the being of God.

The lack of affinity between Calvinism and the Platonist tradition has often been noted. John H. Randall, Jr., writes that the Cambridge Platonists specifically looked to the Platonist tradition for help in their battle against Calvinism.[11] Ernst Cassirer observes that in their opposition to Calvinism, these Cambridge Platonists took essentially the same position that Pelagius adopted against Augustine.[12]

On the one hand Edwards was hampered by his own pantheizing tendencies, which resulted from his Platonism. On the other hand he had to contend with the "ethicizing" tendencies that were already at work all around him. Perhaps he simply came on the scene too late. Herbert Wallace Schneider writes:

> He failed to see the futility of insisting on the Puritan principles. He preached humility to the proud. He tried to awaken a sense of sin in those who were becoming constantly more self-reliant. He defended the glory of God to those who were beginning to revel in their own glory. He believed in submission at a time when his countrymen were raising the cry of independence. He could not stem the current.[13]

History often repeats itself, and therefore one wonders whether twentieth-century Calvinism will eventually follow in the footsteps of New England Calvinism and undergo a similar transformation from within. Much will depend on whether "pantheizing" and "ethicizing" tendencies are allowed to take root. Will God's sovereignty and glory remain central, or will man and his rationality serve as the starting point?

VII

The collapse of New England Calvinism was caused in part by the "ethicizing" process in theology. A change in the concept of God leads to many other changes. Once the doctrine of God's wrath and judgment is denied, a thoroughgoing reinterpretation of Christian doctrine is required.

The question of God's wrath, then, is not a theological issue to be taken lightly. We may not simply dismiss the God of wrath as an inadequate Old Testament foreshadowing of the New Testament God of love. Anthony T. Hanson concludes his book on God's wrath by arguing: "The concept of the wrath of God is therefore one of the great foundation principles of Christian thought. We may call it by other names if we choose, but we attempt to remove it from the New Testament at our peril."[14]

Theologians who retain the concept of God's judgment sometimes interpret it as "the reverse side of grace." Gregory Baum informs us that "there is never any reason for man to be afraid of God." He explains: "God is never one who punishes; God is always Savior. . . ." In that case, what are we to make of Biblical language about God as the Judge who punishes the unrighteousness of man? Baum argues:

> To say that God is a judge who punishes is to impress upon Christians that sin is not simply an evil action in a man's life which he may forget after he has committed it; sin is a source of chaos in the lives of men from which they cannot save themselves. When the bible says that God punishes the wicked, what is announced is the inevitable chain between man's sin and his punishment, as well as the total incapacity of man to save himself from the web of destruction that he has initiated by his sinning.[15]

Baum is out of step with Scripture on two points. First of all, the judgment that rests on man is not *always* his own doing or the result of his own folly but sometimes comes immediately from the hand of God. God does intervene in our lives. Second, judgment is not always a means to work redemption; in some cases judgment is final. God did not send fire down on Sodom to move its wicked inhabitants to repentance.

Christians who take the Bible seriously will detect a clear warning in the passages about judgment. God does bring evil into our lives. Therefore Job declares: "Shall we receive good at the hand of God, and shall we not receive evil?" (Job 2:10). After Job's afflictions end and he is restored to God's favor, we read that his brothers and sisters and friends "showed him sympathy and comforted him for all the evil that the Lord had brought upon him" (Job 42:11). Remember also Amos's question: "Does evil befall a city, unless the Lord has done it?" (Amos 3:6). In a time of great apostasy the Lord said to His people: "I have set my face against this city [Jerusalem] for evil and not for good, says the Lord: it shall be given into the hand of the king of Babylon, and he shall burn it with fire" (Jeremiah 21:10).

VIII

Only if we recognize the reality of judgment and punishment will the doctrine of Christ's crucifixion and atoning death make sense. We saw earlier that John Hick, who approaches the problem of evil by talking about the "God of love," does not know what to make of Christ's suffering and death on the cross (see p. 73 above). Indeed, if God renounces punishment, the cross makes no sense.

J. Gresham Machen comments that there is a great deal of misunderstanding on this point. Those who object to the Christian doctrine of the atonement generally have not understood it:

> The modern liberal teachers persist in speaking of the sacrifice of Christ as though it were a sacrifice made by some one other than God. They speak of it as though it meant that God waits coldly until a price is paid to Him before He forgives sin. As a matter of fact, it means nothing of the kind; the objection ignores that which is absolutely fundamental in the Christian doctrine of the Cross. The fundamental thing is that God Himself, and not another, makes the sacrifice for sin — God Himself in the person of the Son who assumed our nature and died for us, God Himself in the person of the Father who spared not His own Son but offered Him up for us all. Salvation is as free *for us* as the air we breathe; God's the dreadful cost, ours the gain.[16]

It is worth noting that the Christian conception of the place of punishment in human life (see Chapter 13 above) cannot be divorced from the doctrine of the atonement. Frank Pakenham observes that there is a doctrine of retribution behind the idea that God punishes our sin in Christ's sacrificial death on the cross. He argues: ". . . if we eliminate retribution from the criminal code we are likely, in practice, to weaken the belief [in the doctrine of atonement], not only in Christian morals, but in Christian theology."[17]

IX

What conclusions can we draw now that we have come to the end of this exploration? The upshot of the matter, it seems to me, is that sin, together with all the natural evil it leads to, has no place in God's good creation and will surely be rooted out when God's time has come. This much we can say on the basis of Scripture. James Orr expresses this outlook:

Numerous as are the perplexities that still crowd upon us, the master-key to their solution, at least, is given when it is discovered that sin is an alien element in the universe, and that it is balanced, in God's grace by a redemption which means its final overthrow, and the establishment in its room of a Kingdom of God, already begun, growing to triumph, and awaiting its perfection in eternity. Only it is to be acknowledged that our lights on these vast matters are in this life "broken," refracted, partial; that it is but the "outskirts" of God's ways we can discern. [18]

From this perspective we can draw important conclusions about how to live with evil. Herman Bavinck points to the relationship between suffering and punishment when he writes: "Guilt turns suffering into punishment; when guilt is removed, suffering can remain what it is, and yet change completely in character. Death is a fact for believers and unbelievers alike; still, for unbelievers it is a punishment, while for believers it is a passageway to eternal life." [19]

Short of Christ's return, suffering will never be eliminated from our lives. Fortunately, we may live our suffering in God's grace — supported by His goodness and comforted by the knowledge that our pain is not retribution for our sin. Christ has paid the price for us.

What there remains for us to do is to work and wait for Christ's return. We know that His Kingdom will not be established on earth without conflict and strife. Hence we must learn to live with evil during this interim age, bearing in mind the advice of the prophet Isaiah, advice that applies not just to his time but to the entire new dispensation:

> Come, my people, enter your chambers,
> and shut your doors behind you;
> hide yourselves for a little while
> until the wrath is past.
> For behold, the Lord is coming forth out of his place
> to punish the inhabitants of the earth for their iniquity,
> and the earth will disclose the blood shed upon her,
> and will no more cover her slain.
>
> (Isaiah 26:20—21)

POSTSCRIPT

A consideration of the problem of evil sheds light on various philosophical and theological themes and issues and gives rise to some new questions in the process. This study suggests at least these eight themes, issues, or questions.

(1) Many philosophical discussions of the problem of evil are so narrow that they can hardly be said to be treatments of the problem at all. Some philosophers discuss the question whether the proposition affirming evil's existence is compatible with the set of propositions ascribing certain attributes to God. This is indeed an interesting point to pursue, but it hardly qualifies as a discussion of the problem of evil understood as an existential question demanding an answer of every sensitive human being. I suspect that it is the influence of the Platonist tradition that leads some philosophers to suppose that evil need not be dealt with as an existential question at all. When God is conceived of as pure goodness (the Good), the reality of evil fades into insignificance.

(2) In our discussions of the original goodness of the world as God made it, we should pay careful attention to the relation between goodness and perfection and also ask ourselves what — if anything — the words "very good" in Genesis 1:31 have to do with maximal greatness. Perhaps the discussion of Guanilo's perfect island in the context of the debate about Anselm's ontological argument for the existence of God can teach us something about goodness.

(3) It is unfortunately true that the character and status of God's laws and norms for created reality is a neglected theme in Christian philosophy. One does not get far in thinking about the problem of evil without needing to explore this theme. Perhaps the problem of evil can serve to stimulate the further development of Christian philosophy in analyzing the nature of created reality.

(4) The basic decisions made by philosophers and theologians with regard to the question of evil are not purely logical or conceptual or based solely on theoretical considerations. The worldview one holds plays an important role in defining the framework or range of options within which an answer is to be sought. The apparent inability of the Platonist and liberal tradition to deal seriously with evil illustrates this point. The question of the relation between worldviews and philosophical thought is another neglected theme to which Christian philosophy should devote sustained attention.

(5) The only proper worldview for the Christian philosopher to presuppose is the one articulated in Scripture. The theme the Bible presents as the framework for understanding man and his plight in the world is that of creation, fall, and redemption. This theme needs to be carefully distinguished from the conception of man's "fallenness" found among those who view evil as necessary (see Chapter 5 above). It is only when we view man as a creature who was created good but who then decided to pursue a path of sin and destruction that we can make sense of the experience of evil in this world. It is only then that Christ emerges as the sole possibility for man's redemption and restoration to his intended place as the crown of creation.

(6) Goodness is not the most fundamental of ontological categories. Meaning, broadly conceived, is a better place to start. But what about the relationship between meaning and evil? Herman Dooyeweerd writes: "Is sinful reality still *meaning*? Is it not meaningless, or rather the adversary of meaning, since meaning can only exist in the religious dependence on its Origin? Here we indeed touch the deepest problem of Christian philosophy."[1] This line of argument must be balanced against the suggestion made by William James that evil facts "are a genuine portion of reality; and they may after all be the best key to life's significance; and possibly the only openers of our eyes to the deepest levels of truth."[2]

(7) In the light of the liberal principle of continuity (see p. 130 above), which can easily result in a monism embracing both God and the world, Christian theologians and philosophers must be careful not to get carried away in their opposition to false distinctions, which they then brand "dualisms" to be rejected. Not every distinction is a false one; not every duality is

equivalent to a dualism. The making of distinctions is an essential element in theoretical thought. And it is important to remember that orthodox Christianity rests on a fundamental distinction that may never be swept aside — the ontological distinction between Creator and creature.

(8) The problem of evil should not be forgotten when we engage in theological reflection on the "God of love" of whom the Bible speaks. We must ask ourselves: What does it mean to speak theologically of God as "love"? Does such language sometimes make us deaf to important themes in Scripture that also clamor for recognition? John Hick chose a striking title for his treatment of the problem of evil: "Evil and the God of Love." Could one also write on evil and use the title "Evil and the God of Wrath"?

NOTES

INTRODUCTION

1. From a letter of December 31, 1777, quoted in *Gotthold Ephraim Lessing in Selbstzeugnissen und Bilddokumenten*, ed. Wolfgang Drews (Reinbek bei Hamburg: Rowohlt, 1962), p. 137.

2. *The World as Will and Representation*, trans. E. F. J. Payne (New York: Dover Publications, 1966), I, 324.

3. "On Suicide," in his *Essays: Moral, Political and Literary* (London: Oxford University Press, 1963), p. 595.

4. *The Grapes of Wrath* (New York: Viking Press, 1939), p. 32.

CHAPTER 1: NATURAL EVIL

1. *Dialogues Concerning Natural Religion*, ed. John Valdimir Price (Oxford: Clarendon Press, 1976), part 10, pp. 221—222.

2. *Essays on Ethics, Religion and Society*, Vol. X of the *Collected Works of John Stuart Mill* (Toronto: University of Toronto Press; London: Routledge and Kegan Paul, 1969), p. 385.

3. See *God and Human Anguish* (Nashville: Abingdon Press, 1977), pp. 10, 14; see also pp. 16, 201, 229.

4. *Oration on the Dignity of Man*, trans. E. L. Forbes, in *The Renaissance Philosophy of Man*, ed. Ernst Cassirer, P. O. Kristeller, and J. H. Randall, Jr. (Chicago: University of Chicago Press, 1948), pp. 224—225.

5. *The Financier*, ch. 1.

6. *Birds in Town and Village* (London and Toronto: J. M. Dent & Sons; and New York: E. P. Dutton & Co., 1923), pp. 102—103.

7. *Far Away and Long Ago: A History of My Early Life* (London and Toronto: J. M. Dent & Sons; and New York: E. P. Dutton & Co., 1923), pp. 41—42.

CHAPTER 2: MORAL EVIL

1. *Civilization and Its Discontents*, trans. James Strachey (New York: W. W. Norton & Company, 1962), pp. 65—66, 69.

2. *Collected Writings of John Murray*, Vol. II: *Select Lectures in Systematic Theology* (Edinburgh: The Banner of Truth Trust, 1977), 77, 72.

3. *Aspects of Liberalism* (Grand Rapids: Eerdmans, 1951), p. 119.

4. *Our Reasonable Faith*, trans. Henry Zylstra (Grand Rapids: Baker Book House, 1977), p. 247.

5. *Our Reasonable Faith*, p. 229.

CHAPTER 3: DEMONIC EVIL

1. *The Reality of the Devil* (New York: Harper and Row, 1972), p. xi.

2. *Paul Tillich's Philosophy of Culture, Science, and Religion* (New York: Harper and Row, 1965), p. 230.

3. *Evil and the God of Love*, revised edition (New York: Harper and Row, 1978), p. 13.

4. See *Gereformeerde Dogmatiek* (Kampen: J. H. Kok, 1928—1930), III, 128.

5. "Evangelicalism and the Mennonite Tradition," in *Evangelicalism and Anabaptism*, ed. C. Norman Kraus (Scottdale, Pa., and Kitchener, Ont.: Herald Press, 1979), p. 166.

6. *The Gulag Archipelago*, trans. Thomas P. Whitney (New York: Harper and Row, 1974), I, 168.

7. *Gereformeerde Dogmatiek*, III, 128.

8. *Christianity and the Occult* (Chicago: Moody Press, 1972), p. 36.

9. *The Devil's Share: An Essay on the Diabolic in Modern Society*, trans. Haakon Chevalier (New York: Meridian Books, 1956), p. 33.

10. *Satan and His Gospel* (Swengel, Pennsylvania: Bible Truth Depot, 1917), pp. 50, 52.

11. In *Mystery, Magic and Miracle*, ed. Edward F. Heenan (Englewood Cliffs, N.J.: Prentice-Hall, 1973), pp. 95, 90, 96—97.

12. *Witchcraft in the Middle Ages* (Ithaca, N.Y.: Cornell University Press, 1972), p. 20.

13. *Systematic Theology* (rpt. Grand Rapids: Eerdmans, 1979), I, 647.

14. *Gereformeerde Dogmatiek*, II, 410.

15. James Kallas, *The Real Satan: From Biblical Times to the Present* (Minneapolis: Augsburg Publishing House, 1975), pp. 107—108.

16. *Christian Faith: An Introduction to the Study of the Faith*, trans. Sierd Woudstra (Grand Rapids: Eerdmans, 1979), p. 176.

CHAPTER 4: EVIL AS ULTIMATE: MANICHAEISM

1. Geo Widengren, *Mani and Manichaeism* (London: Weidenfeld and Nicolson, 1965), p. 139.

2. See Widengren, pp. 43—44.

3. *Augustine of Hippo* (Berkeley: University of California Press, 1967), pp. 47, 50.

4. *Marcion and His Influence* (London: S.P.C.K., 1948), p. 71.

5. *Marcion and His Influence*, p. 123.

6. *Christ and Culture* (New York: Harper and Brothers, 1951), pp. 189, 188; see also pp. 174—175.

7. *The Social Teaching of the Christian Churches*, trans. Olive Wyon (rpt. New York: Harper and Row, 1960), pp. 605—606.

CHAPTER 5: EVIL AS NECESSARY: HEGEL AND SCHLEIERMACHER

1. *Sin Comes of Age* (Philadelphia: Westminster Press, 1975), pp. 24, 26, 27.

2. *Pragmatism and the Tragic Sense of Life* (New York: Basic Books, 1974), p. 18.

3. *God in Modern Philosophy* (Chicago: Henry Regnery Company, 1967), pp. 230, 231.

4. *The Religious Dimension in Hegel's Thought* (Bloomington: Indiana University Press, 1967), pp. 131—132.

5. *A Philosophy of Religion* (Englewood Cliffs, N.J.: Prentice-Hall, 1940), pp. 245—246.

6. *God and Human Anguish* (see Ch. 1, n. 3), pp. 248, 246.

7. *Schleiermacher on Christ and Religion: A New Introduction* (New York: Charles Scribner's Sons, 1964), p. 204.

8. *Friedrich Schleiermacher* (Waco, Texas: Word Books, 1979), p. 117.

9. *Evil and the God of Love* (see Ch. 3, n. 3), p. 210.

10. *Evil and the God of Love*, pp. 286, 231ff.

11. *Evil and the God of Love*, p. 259.

12. *Evil and the God of Love*, pp. 248—249.

13. *Evil and the God of Love*, pp. 249—250.

14. See *Evil and the God of Love*, p. 255.

CHAPTER 6: EVIL AS NON-BEING: THE PLATONIST TRADITION

1. *The Works of Ralph Waldo Emerson* (New York: Bigelow, Brown and Co., no date), I, 52.

2. *Works*, IV, 492.

3. "An Address to the Senior Class in Divinity College, Cambridge," in *Works*, IV, 87.

4. *The Problem of Evil*, trans. Christopher Williams (New York: Hawthorn Books, 1959), pp. 76—77, 8; see also pp. 71ff., 128.

5. *Renaissance Thought: The Classic, Scholastic, and Humanist Strains* (New York: Harper and Row, 1961), p. 48.

6. *Friedrich Schleiermacher* (see Ch. 5, n. 8), p. 86; see also Robert R. Williams, *Schleiermacher the Theologian: The Construction of the Doctrine of God* (Philadelphia: Fortress Press, 1978), pp. 14, 57ff., 141, 148. Williams identifies the Platonism of Schleiermacher with the tradition of Nikolaus Cusanus.

7. *Protagoras*, 358, in *The Dialogues of Plato*, trans. B. Jowett (New York: Random House, 1937), I, 127.

8. *Being, Nothing and God* (Assen, the Netherlands: Van Gorcum, 1970), p. 59.

9. *Neoplatonism* (New York: Charles Scribner's Sons, 1972), p. 160.

10. *Augustine of Hippo* (see Ch. 4, n. 3), p. 99; see also pp. 51—53.

11. *The Interpretation of Religion* (New York and Nashville: Abingdon Press, no date; first published 1928), p. 399.

12. *Plotinus and Neoplatonism* (Cambridge: Bowes & Bowes, 1952), pp. 129—130.

13. *Augustine: Philosopher of Freedom* (New York: Desclée Company, 1958), p. 147.

14. "Optimism," *Philosophical Dictionary*, in *Candide and Other Writings*, ed. Haskell M. Block (New York: Modern Library, no date), p. 423.

15. *The Philosophy of Plotinus* (London: Longmans, Green & Co., 1948), II, 172.

16. *Personal Idealism and Mysticism* (London: Longmans, Green & Co., 1913), p. 25.

17. *The Philosophy of Plotinus*, I, 22.

18. *Personal Idealism and Mysticism*, p. vi.

19. See Clark, *Augustine: Philosopher of Freedom*, p. 153.

20. *Christian Mysticism* (London: Methuen & Co., 1899), p. 107n; see also p. 321, and *Personal Idealism and Mysticism*, pp. 35, 37, 59.

21. *Theists and Atheists: A Typology of Non-Belief* (The Hague: Mouton Publishers, 1980), pp. 15—16.

22. *Gereformeerde Dogmatiek* (see Ch. 3, n. 4), II, 370.

23. *E Voto Dordraceno: Toelichting op den Heidelbergschen Catechismus* (Amsterdam: J. A. Wormser, 1892—1895), I, 149—150.

24. *E Voto Dordraceno*, II, 15.

25. *Augustine: Philosopher of Freedom*, pp. 144—145.

26. *Systematic Theology* (see Ch. 3, n. 13), II, 136; see also 133—134.

CHAPTER 7: EVIL AS ALIENATION FROM GOD: AUGUSTINE AND CALVIN

1. *Personal Idealism and Mysticism* (see Ch. 6, n. 16), p. 56; see also pp. 86—87, 128.

2. *The Platonic Tradition in Anglo-Saxon Philosophy* (London: George Allen & Unwin; and New York: Macmillan, 1931), p. 26.

3. *Renaissance Thought* (see Ch. 6, n. 5), p. 55.

4. "The Anti-Manichaean Writings," in *A Companion to the Study of St. Augustine*, ed. Roy W. Battenhouse (New York: Oxford University Press, 1955), p. 168.

5. *The Retractations*, trans. Sister Mary Ines Bogan (Washington, D.C.: Catholic University of America Press, 1968; Vol. LX of *The Fathers of the Church*), 1.1.4.

6. See *St. Augustine and Christian Platonism* (Villanova, Pa.: Villanova University Press, 1967; The Saint Augustine Lecture for 1966), pp. 24ff. This lecture has been reprinted in *Augustine: A Collection of Critical Essays*, ed. R. A. Markus (Garden City, N.Y.: Anchor Books, 1972), pp. 3—37.

7. *Christian Faith and Greek Philosophy* (London: Darton, Longman & Todd, 1960), p. 68.

8. *The City of God*, trans. Gerald G. Walsh and Grace Monahan (Washington, D.C.: Catholic University of America Press, 1952; Vol. XIV of *The Fathers of the Church*), 11.15.

9. *Our Reasonable Faith* (see Ch. 2, n. 4), p. 249.

10. *Gereformeerde Dogmatiek* (see Ch. 3, n. 4), III, 117, 133.

11. *E Voto Dordraceno* (see Ch. 6, n. 23), I, 436.

12. *The Development of St. Augustine from Neoplatonism to Christianity, 386—391 A.D.* (Washington, D.C.: University Press of America, 1980), p. 175.

13. *Institutes of the Christian Religion*, 2 vols., trans. Ford Lewis Battles and ed. John T. McNeill (Philadelphia: Westminster Press, 1960; Vols. XX and XXI of *The Library of Christian Classics*), 2.16.11.

14. *Institutes*, 2.12.1.

15. *Theists and Atheists* (see Ch. 6, n. 21), p. 11; see also pp. 16, 18—19, 25.

16. *Christian Faith* (see Ch. 3, n. 16), p. 153.

17. *Saint Augustine on Personality* (New York: Macmillan, 1960; The Saint Augustine Lecture for 1959), pp. 42, 5.

18. *The City of God* (Washington, D.C.: Catholic University of America Press, 1954; Vol. XXIV of *The Fathers of the Church*), 16.27.

19. See *Gereformeerde Dogmatiek*, II, 528ff.

20. *Institutes*, 2.12.1, 2.2.1.

CHAPTER 8: DIMENSIONS OF EVIL

1. *Illness as Metaphor* (New York: Farrar, Straus & Giroux, 1978), p. 82.

2. *Illness as Metaphor*, pp. 56—57.

3. *Gereformeerde Dogmatiek* (see Ch. 3, n. 4), III, 160; see also II, 443.

4. *Gereformeerde Dogmatiek*, III, 1.

5. *Gereformeerde Dogmatiek*, II, 526.

6. *Tusschen "Ja" und "Neen"* (Kampen: J. H. Kok, 1929), p. 133.

7. *Gereformeerde Dogmatiek*, III, 39.

8. *Faith, Hope and Charity*, trans. Bernard M. Peebles (Washington: Catholic University of America Press, 1947; Vol. II of *The Fathers of the Church*), 8.27.

9. *The City of God* (see Ch. 7, nn. 8 and 18), 22.1.

10. *Gereformeerde Dogmatiek*, III, 34.

11. *E Voto Dordraceno* (see Ch. 6, n. 23), I, 68.

12. *Gereformeerde Dogmatiek*, II, 538.

13. *Gereformeerde Dogmatiek,* III, 155.

14. *Gereformeerde Dogmatiek,* III, 40—41.

15. *Collected Writings of John Murray,* (see Ch. 2, n. 2), II, 67.

16. *Systematic Theology* (see Ch. 3, n. 13), I, 436.

17. *Institutes* (see Ch. 7, n. 13), 3.23.2.

18. "The Last Event and Its Picture of God," in *Contemporary Accents in Liberal Religion,* ed. Bradford E. Gale (Boston: Beacon Press, 1960), pp. 148, 149.

19. *Philosophy of Religion* (Englewood Cliffs, N.J.: Prentice-Hall, 1963), p. 40; *Evil and the God of Love* (see Ch. 3, n. 3), p. 243.

20. *Evil and the God of Love,* pp. 249, 125.

21. *A Genetic History of the New England Theology* (Chicago: University of Chicago Press, 1907), pp. 8, 547.

22. *The Puritan Mind* (New York: Henry Holt and Company, 1930), p. 201.

23. *De Vleeschwording des Woords* (Amsterdam: J. A. Wormser, 1887), p. 231.

24. See *The Sovereignty of Grace* (Phillipsburg, N.J.: Presbyterian and Reformed Publishing Company, 1979), pp. 19, 21, 46, 86.

CHAPTER 9: PORNOGRAPHY AND VIOLENCE

1. "Against Pornography," in *Perspectives on Pornography,* ed. Douglas A. Hughes (New York: St. Martin's Press, 1970), p. 74.

2. *The Other Victorians: A Study of Sexuality and Pornography in Mid-Nineteenth-Century England* (New York: Bantam Books, 1967), pp. 281, 272.

3. "The Pornographic Imagination," in *Styles of Radical Will* (New York: Farrar, Straus & Giroux, 1969), p. 46.

4. "The Pornographic Imagination," pp. 47—48.

5. *The Mind Possessed: A Physiology of Possession, Mysticism and Faith Healing* (Philadelphia: J. B. Lippincott Company, 1974), p. 86.

6. "Against Pornography," p. 86.

7. *The Erotic Minorities,* trans. Anselm Hollo (New York: Grove Pres, 1966), pp. 69, 102.

8. *The Erotic Minorities,* p. 84; see also pp. 61, 86—87.

CHAPTER 10: SUFFERING AND SYMPATHY

1. *The Face of Battle* (New York: Viking Press, 1976), p. 20.

2. *Born of Those Years: An Autobiography* (New York: Henry Holt and Company, 1951), p. 31.

3. *Old Age,* trans. Patrick O'Brian (London: André Deutsch and Weidenfeld & Nicolson, 1972), p. 1.

4. See Jean-François Steiner, *Treblinka,* trans. Helen Weaver (London: Corgi Books, 1969), p. 413.

5. I have dealt with this mode of knowledge in my book *Historical*

Understanding in the Thought of Wilhelm Dilthey (Toronto: University of Toronto Press, 1980). See especially chs. 5 and 6.

6. "The Conspiracy of Silence," in *Pastoral Care of the Dying and Bereaved: Selected Readings*, ed. Robert B. Reeves, Jr., Robert E. Neale, and Austin H. Kutscher (New York: Health Sciences Publishing Corp., 1973), p. 49.

7. "The Son of Man Must Suffer," in *The Mystery of Suffering and Death*, ed. Michael J. Taylor (New York: Alba House, 1973), p. 35.

8. "The Son of Man Must Suffer," p. 43.

CHAPTER 11: CONFLICT AND SPECTACLE

1. *The Fabulous Showman: The Life and Times of P. T. Barnum* (New York: Alfred A. Knopf, 1959), p. 98.

2. See Leslie Fiedler, *Freaks: Myths and Images of the Secret Self* (New York: Simon and Schuster, 1978).

3. See *Roman Life and Manners Under the Early Empire*, vol. 2 (London: George Routledge & Sons; and New York: E. P. Dutton & Co., 1936), pp. 71, 72.

4. *The Warriors: Reflections on Men in Battle* (New York: Harper and Row, 1973), p. 39; see also pp. 33ff.

5. *The Warriors*, p. 38.

6. Wilhelm Prüller, *Diary of a German Soldier*, ed. H. C. Robbins Landon and Sebastian Leitner (New York: Coward-McCann, 1963), pp. 71, 107; see also pp. 23, 29, 67, 69, 73, 82, 89, 120.

7. Cornelius Ryan, *The Longest Day: June 6, 1944* (New York: Simon and Schuster, 1959), pp. 89–90.

8. See *A Handbook of Literature*, by William Flint Thrall and Addison Hibbard, revised and enlarged by C. Hugh Holman (Indianapolis: Odyssey Press, 1960), p. 105.

9. *The Anti-Society: An Account of the Victorian Underworld* (Boston: Gambit, 1970), p. 14.

10. *The Christian View of God and the World as Centring in the Incarnation*, 7th ed. (New York: Charles Scribner's Sons, 1904), p. 194.

CHAPTER 12: IMAGINATION AND DEPICTION

1. *Heroes, Hero Worship and the Heroic in History* (New York: A. L. Burt Company, no date), pp. 17, 13.

2. *The Pornography of Power* (Chicago: Quadrangle Books, 1968), pp. 81–82, 135.

3. *The City of God* (see Ch. 7, nn. 8 and 18), 14.19.

4. *The City of God*, 14.23.

5. *The City of God*, 14.23.

6. "Against Pornography" (see Ch. 9, n. 1), pp. 74–75. The definition is italicized in the original.

CHAPTER 13: PUNISHMENT AND MORAL EDUCATION

1. *Sin as a Problem of To-day* (London: Hodder and Stoughten, 1910), p. 271.

2. *Punishing Criminals: Concerning a Very Old and Painful Question* (New York: Basic Books, 1975), p. 8.

3. *Sin as a Problem of To-day*, p. 166.

4. In H. B. Action, et al., *Punishment: For and Against* (New York: Hart Publishing Company, 1971), p. 145.

5. In *Punishment: For and Against*, pp. 80—81.

6. In *Punishment: For and Against*, p. 129.

7. *The Story of Punishment: A Record of Man's Inhumanity to Man*, 2nd ed. (Montclair, N.J.: Patterson Smith, 1972), pp. 265—266; see also p. 270.

8. *The Story of Punishment*, p. 280.

9. *The Idea of Punishment* (London: Geoffrey Chapman, 1961), pp. 47—48.

10. See *De straf: Haar ethisch en psychologisch aspect* (Kampen: J. H. Kok, 1956), p. 55.

11. *Hegel's Philosophy of Right*, trans. T. M. Knox (London: Oxford University Press, 1967), p. 71.

12. In *Punishment: For and Against*, pp. 53—54.

13. *Punishing Criminals*, p. 186.

14. *The Shape of Religious Instruction* (Dayton, Ohio: Pflaum, 1971), pp. 312, 302.

15. "The Teaching of Religion," in *Toward a Future for Religious Education*, ed. James Michael Lee and Patrick C. Rooney (Dayton, Ohio: Pflaum Press, 1970), p. 67. This passage is italicized in the original.

16. *The Flow of Religious Instruction: A Social-Science Approach* (Dayton, Ohio: Pflaum/Standard, 1973), p. 22.

17. "Toward a New Era: A Blueprint for Positive Action," in *The Religious Education We Need: Toward the Renewal of Christian Education*, ed. James Michael Lee (Mishawaka, Indiana: Religious Education Press, 1977), p. 127.

18. See *The Flow of Religious Education*, pp. 289—290.

19. "Toward a New Era," pp. 125—126.

20. *The Shape of Religious Instruction*, p. 4

21. *The Flow of Religious Instruction*, p. 292.

22. *The Flow of Religious Instruction*, p. 196.

23. *The Flow of Religious Instruction*, p. 291.

24. "Toward a New Era," p. 123.

25. *The Flow of Religious Instruction*, pp. 275—276.

26. *Educating for Responsible Action* (Grand Rapids: Eerdmans and CSI Publications, 1980), p. 14.

27. *Educating for Responsible Action*, pp. 13—14.

28. *Educating for Responsible Action*, p. 116.

29. *Educating for Responsible Action*, p. 15.

30. *Educating for Responsible Action*, p. vi.

31. *The Rebirth of Ministry: A Study of the Biblical Character of the Church's Ministry* (Philadelphia: Westminster Press, no date), pp. 100—101.

CHAPTER 14: THE LIBERAL MIND

1. *Suicide of the West: An Essay on the Meaning and Destiny of Liberalism* (New York: The John Day Company, 1964), p. 118.

2. "The Mistake Liberals Make," in *The Case Against Pornography*, ed. David Holbrook (La Salle, Illinois: Open Court, 1973), p. 265.

3. *Christianity and Liberalism* (Grand Rapids: Eerdmans, 1923), p. 136.

4. "From Anguish to Liberty: Faith of a Liberal Revolutionary," in *This Is My Philosophy*, ed. Whit Burnet (New York: Harper and Brothers, 1957), pp. 329—330.

5. "From Anguish to Liberty," p. 331.

6. "The Crisis of Liberalism," in *Essays with a Purpose* (London: Hollis and Carter, 1954), p. 22.

7. *The Impact of American Religious Liberalism* (New York: Harper and Row, 1962), p. 209.

8. *The Impact of American Religious Liberalism*, p. 9.

9. *Christianity and Liberalism*, pp. 62—63.

10. *Christianity and Liberalism*, p. 63.

11. *Christianity and Liberalism*, p. 64.

12. See *Christianity and Liberalism*, p. 2.

13. *Christianity and Liberalism*, p. 155.

14. *The Liberal Mind* (New York: Vintage Books, 1968), p. 86.

15. *Liberalism: Its Meaning and History* (Princeton: D. Van Nostrand, 1958), p. 12.

16. *Suicide of the West*, p. 65.

17. *The Liberal Mind*, p. 131.

CHAPTER 15: JUDGMENT AND THE COMING KINGDOM

1. *The Beginnings of Unitarianism in America* (Boston: Beacon Press, 1955), pp. 6, 10.

2. *Christian Faith and Greek Philosophy* (see Ch. 7, n. 7), p. 68.

3. See *St. Augustine and Christian Platonism* (see Ch. 7, n. 6), pp. 24—26.

4. "The Moral Argument Against Calvinism," in *The Works of William E. Channing* (1882; rpt. New York: Burt Franklin, 1970), pp. 461, 462.

5. "The Moral Argument Against Calvinism," p. 468.

6. See *The Puritan Pronaos: Studies in the Intellectual Life of New England in the Seventeenth Century* (New York: New York University Press, 1936), p. 10.

7. *Harvard College in the Seventeenth Century* (Cambridge: Harvard University Press, 1936), p. 276.

8. *The Philosophical Theology of Jonathan Edwards* (New York: Columbia University Press, 1960), pp. 30, 6.

9. *Beauty and Sensibility in the Thought of Jonathan Edwards* (New Haven and London: Yale University Press, 1968), p. 118.

10. *Jonathan Edwards* (New York: Harper and Brothers, 1932), p. 188.

11. See *The Career of Philosophy*, Vol. I: *From the Middle Ages to the Enlightenment* (New York: Columbia University Press, 1962), pp. 471, 479.

12. See *The Platonic Renaissance in England*, trans. James P. Pettegrove (Austin: University of Texas Press, 1953), p. 82.

13. *The Puritan Mind* (see Ch. 8, n. 22), p. 155.

14. *The Wrath of the Lamb* (London: S.P.C.K., 1957), p. 201.

15. "Does God Punish?" in *Does God Punish?*, ed. Richard McCarthy (Glen Rock, N.J.: Paulist Press, 1968), pp. 21, 14, 16—17.

16. *Christianity and Liberalism* (see Ch. 14, n. 3), p. 132.

17. See *The Idea of Punishment* (see Ch. 13, n. 9), pp. 55—56.

18. *Sin as a Problem of To-day* (see Ch. 13, n. 1), p. 311.

19. *Gereformeerde Dogmatiek* (see Ch. 3, n. 4), III, 150.

POSTSCRIPT

1. *A New Critique of Theoretical Thought*, trans. David H. Freeman and H. de Jongste (Philadelphia: Presbyterian and Reformed Publishing Company, 1955), I, 33.

2. *The Varieties of Religious Experience* (New York: Modern Library, no date), p. 160.

INDEX

159

N